BOGGY CREEK CASEBOOK

Fouke Monster Encounters
1908 to Present

LYLE BLACKBURN

legend
SCAPE

FIRST TIME IN PRINT

An Original Publication of LegendScape Publishing

Boggy Creek Casebook:
Fouke Monster Encounters 1908 to Present

Copyright © 2020 by Lyle Blackburn

ISBN: 978-1-7349206-1-1

Cover art and illustrations by D.W. Frydendall

Photos courtesy of individual photographers as credited

Edited by Beth Wojiski (www.bethwojiski.com)

Proofreading by Craig Woolheater

Print design by Lyle Blackburn

For more information about the author, visit:

    www.lyleblackburn.com
    www.facebook.com/lyleblackburn.official
    www.twitter.com/BlackburnLyle
    www.instagram.com/lyleblackburn

For more information about the artist, visit:

    www.dfrydendall.net
    www.instagram.com/dwfrydendall

For the latest on the Fouke Monster, visit: www.foukemonster.net

This book contains real accounts by credible eyewitnesses

Acknowledgements

This book is dedicated to the amazing people of Fouke, Arkansas. Without their support and assistance, a book like this would not be possible. Over the years, they have entertained my historical pursuits by inviting me into their homes and businesses to share their personal stories. And for that I am forever grateful. Their hospitality and friendship has been one of the most rewarding aspects of my Boggy Creek journey.

Thanks also to the following colleagues and friends who assisted with the research and creation of this book:

John Attaway, Pamula Pierce Barcelou, Ashley Boggs, D.W. Frydendall, Bobby Hamilton, Jerry Hestand, Bryan Impey, Frank McFerrin, Terry Purvis, Denny Roberts, Rickie Roberts, Tom Shirley (RIP), Lon Strickler, Jim Whitehead, Beth Wojiski, and Craig Woolheater.

A special thanks to Jim Powell and the *Texarkana Gazette* for documenting the early wave of sightings, my late friend Smokey Crabtree for all he did to investigate and preserve the stories, and the late Charles B. Pierce and Earl Smith for making *The Legend of Boggy Creek*.

And most of all, I would like to thank all the eyewitnesses and organizations who graciously shared their experiences. Their contributions reside at the heart of this legendary case.

Contents

"If you're ever driving down in our country along about sundown, keep an eye on the dark woods as you cross the Sulphur River bottoms… you may catch a glimpse of a huge, hairy creature watching you from the shadows."

- *The Legend of Boggy Creek*

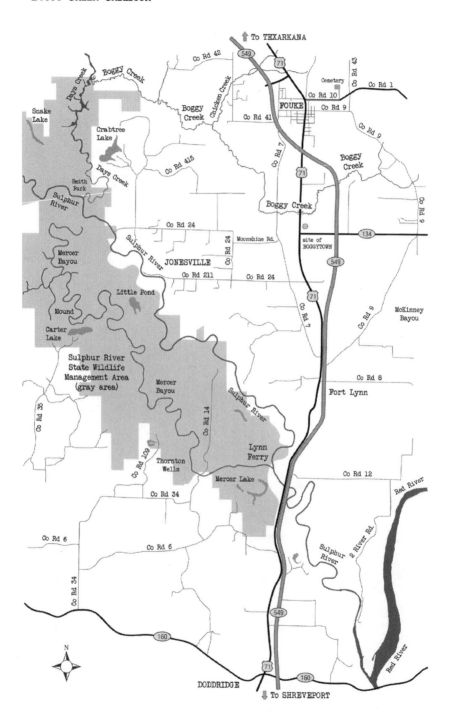

Foreword

Jerry Hestand
- July 2020

In March 2004, several members of a Bigfoot research group and I were conducting an investigation in Fouke, Arkansas, home of the legendary Fouke Monster. Our group was known as the Texas Bigfoot Research Center, and we had been given a report about a coon hunter who had an encounter with an ape-like beast while hunting one night in nearby Mercer Bayou. Our team had arranged to meet the man at a local convenience store in Fouke called the Monster Mart.

As I entered the store, I realized how excited I was to be in the home of the Fouke Monster. This Bigfoot-like creature had been sighted around this small Arkansas town for many years and was the subject of one of my favorite movies of all time, *The Legend of Boggy Creek*. The movie had ignited my interest in Bigfoot when I was just a teenager. Being in Fouke was literally a lifelong dream come true.

It was also a dream come true to be a member of a serious Bigfoot research organization and to have been assigned to collect reports in Miller County, Arkansas. Up to that point, I had investigated a handful of sightings, which I detailed in reports to be published on our website. Talking to witnesses who claimed to have had encounters with the creature fueled my passion even more.

That weekend, we talked to the hunter about his encounter

with the mysterious creature in the bayou. He was a credible witness, and his story sounded plausible. He told us the location of the incident, but would not go there again, even in daylight. Whatever he saw certainly had an effect on him.

Over the years we conducted other investigations in Miller County—enough that I became convinced there were strange creatures inhabiting the Sulphur River Bottoms around Fouke. The others and I knew how important the Fouke Monster story was. This legend had been the basis for so many Bigfoot researchers to begin their hobby in the first place. It is certainly the most important account of a Bigfoot-type creature in the South and perhaps one of the most important and influential in the entire United States. I have traveled across the country, and invariably most of the Bigfoot enthusiasts I've met tell me *The Legend of Boggy Creek* was one of the main inspirations behind their interest in the Bigfoot phenomenon.

A few years after our group investigated the coon hunter incident, we were holding a public meeting in Texarkana, just outside of Fouke. A young man dressed in black was in attendance. He seemed extremely interested in the Bigfoot phenomenon, and in particular the stories surrounding Boggy Creek. After the meeting, the young man introduced himself as Lyle Blackburn. He told me he was planning to write a book about the Fouke Monster and wanted to know if I would like to help him. Of course! Finally, I found someone as interested in the Fouke Monster as I am!

Little did I know my meeting with Lyle would be the start of a series of events that would intertwine me in "The Legend" far more than I could have ever imagined. Over the next few months and years, I accompanied Lyle on many trips to Fouke as he interviewed witness after witness in the small community. Lyle found several sighting locations in the swamps and bayous that we also explored, not to mention locating some of the spots seen in *The Legend of Boggy Creek* movie. These were undoubtedly some of the most exciting years of my life as we examined every facet of our favorite legend.

The end result was Lyle's fantastic, debut book, *The Beast of Boggy Creek*. Finally, there was a book that recounted the incredible history of the Fouke Monster and the making of *The Legend of Boggy Creek*. From then on, Lyle continued to research and write about the "Beast of Boggy Creek," as he became the go-to guy for information regarding the Fouke Monster.

Now Lyle has decided to publish a casebook that contains every Fouke Monster-related sighting, and I couldn't be more pleased. The accounts contained in this book are truly, in my opinion, the most comprehensive listing of information about one of the most iconic Bigfoot mysteries of all time. If not for Lyle's extensive effort to investigate and research the hidden mysteries of the Fouke Monster, I'm afraid many of these stories would have been lost forever.

Looking back at my first meeting with Lyle, we've come a long way. He has truly done the mystery justice by investigating all aspects of the story and distilling these amazing encounters into one complete source. I invite you to sit back and read from cover to cover, or if you like, skip to a particular era and read a favorite report you may have heard of. And if you decide to visit Fouke someday, be sure to keep your eyes on the woods if you find yourself driving in the area just before dark. You never know when YOU may have a frightening encounter to add to the others!

Jerry Hestand

Introduction

Not everything in this world can be explained in simple terms. This is one of those cases. For more than a century now, residents in and around the small town of Fouke, Arkansas, have reported sightings of a strange, ape-like creature that seemingly lives among their woods and waterways. Descriptions are similar to that of a Bigfoot, yet this creature seems a bit more hairy, unkempt, and perhaps scary. It's said to be tall and muscular with matted hair covering its body and much of its face. It appears to be ape-like, yet has the ability to walk upright like a man. Within its facial features and deep-set eyes, there appears to be something eerily human. It is always elusive and sometimes aggressive. In some cases, locals claimed it killed their livestock and even tried to break into their homes. Reports like these have earned the alleged creature—or creatures—a reputation for being dangerous. It is a phenomenon that is equally chilling as it is mysterious.

The ostensible creature in this case has come to be known as the "Fouke Monster." The name was established by a newspaper reporter in 1971 when a wave of dramatic encounters began to make headlines. The creature was nothing new to the locals, however. In the decades preceding the publicized reports, those living in the Sulphur River Bottoms south of town were already referring to the thing as the "Jonesville Monster." And prior to that, hunters and settlers in the area whispered of an ape-like wild man that had no name at all.

Skeptics tend to dismiss these reports as tall tales, hoaxes, or fabrications, yet the locals and other witnesses insist they have seen something that is most assuredly real. Many of the witnesses are prominent citizens, skilled hunters, and even police officials, whose reputations lend credibility to a phenomenon that is undeniably controversial. Some of the sightings have certainly been distant and brief—allowing for the possibility of misidentification—yet many are close enough that witnesses can be confident in their assessment. The encounters may be hard to fathom in today's world, but they are certainly not the result of mass hallucinations or a century-long conspiracy to create a local monster.

In the 1970s, the Fouke Monster reached the heights of notoriety when it became the subject of a feature film, *The Legend of Boggy Creek*. Directed by Texarkana resident, Charles B. Pierce, the movie was originally conceived as a documentary, but ended up as something of a pseudo-documentary horror film that dramatizes the actual events surrounding the Fouke case. The movie went on to become a bona fide box office sensation as it played for years in the theater and drive-in circuits and on television. The unlikely success resulted in the "Boggy Creek Monster" becoming a household name across America and beyond.

Though solid proof of the creature remains elusive, the body of anecdotal reports and occasional footprint finds that have amassed over the last century suggest there is something tangible behind the now-famous legend. Whatever may be lurking in the vast Sulphur River Bottoms has yet to be explained. It might be part of the greater mystery of Bigfoot, and it might be something altogether unique, but either way it has become a significant cornerstone in the roster of American cryptid cases; a case worthy of documenting in detail.

The reports contained in this book comprise all of the ones I've collected and/or researched to date, but surely this work cannot encompass the total extent of the sightings. Not everyone is willing to share an experience that may result in ridicule or is perhaps emotionally upsetting. Seeing something so unusual and startling can have varied effects on people. The reports compiled in this book are the ones I deemed most credible to the best of my ability. A few of the witnesses have asked to remain anonymous, yet most are willing to share their real names because they stand behind what they've experienced. As a nonbiased journalist, I must accept not all of these witnesses may have seen an undiscovered, undocumented creature. However, if any one of them did, then the Fouke Monster is as real as you and I.

1.

Early Encounters

When *The Legend of Boggy Creek* movie went into wide distribution across American theaters in 1973, it established the Fouke Monster as a certified sensation. The alleged creature had been discussed for more than a year in regional newspapers, but the medium of film helped spread the details of the reported incidents much further and faster than the printed source ever could. As a result, most people's knowledge of the case came directly from the movie, which is fairly accurate in its dramatizations but does not offer much in the way of specific dates or time frames.

Though it was not explicitly stated, the movie portrayed Fouke Monster incidents from approximately 1954 to 1971. This timeline, along with the movie's plot, left viewers with the impression the creature had suddenly surfaced in the 1940s or '50s and had disappeared shortly after the heyday of encounters in the 1970s. However, local reports and other research have established a much longer history of incidents that date back to at least 1908 in the Fouke area and even further back if including general "wild man" sightings in Arkansas and its neighboring states.

The fact the creature (or creatures) have been reported for a much longer period only seems natural, since if it does indeed exist, then it would surely have been seen prior to the 1950s. And that's exactly the case. Though it's difficult to pinpoint the very first sighting, tales of such a creature in the bottomlands surrounding Fouke can be dated to a time in the early 1900s when people were settling in the area and moving about in its woods and swamps. As homesteaders moved in, perhaps they were the first since Native Americans to encounter the mysteries that have lingered in this area for more than a century now.

This section details the early sightings on record, gleaned from various sources such as newspapers, local stories, and personal interviews. These mysterious incidents were the first to suggest that perhaps there is some sort of creature living in Southern Arkansas that we have yet to identify or understand. And while there were probably just as many encounters that were never told or ultimately lost to the whispers of time, this is enough to establish a rather lengthy history for a creature who would later become known as the Fouke Monster.

The First

1908 - Mercer Bayou

In an article printed in the August 23, 1973, *Victoria Advocate* newspaper, Fouke resident Willie Smith claimed his sister saw the creature around 1908 when she was ten years old. There are no details regarding the nature of the sighting, but after further research and interviews with the locals, I discovered the sister Smith referred to is Kate Savell. I had heard of Kate's sighting, and when I mentioned Smith's claim to a friend in Fouke, I was told his sister and this woman were one and the same. According to the story, Kate had accompanied her family on a fishing trip to Mercer Bayou (a swampy area south of town). While she was playing in the nearby woods, she noticed a hairy, man-like animal watching her from behind some bushes. It quickly disappeared into the shadows and was not seen again.

FOUKE FACTS: During my early research into the case, I spoke to other anonymous sources who claim someone else—possibly a member of their own family—was the source of this sighting, dating it at around the same time, between the years of 1904 and 1910. Understandably, it is hard to pin down an exact date or a precise recollection a century later, but suffice to say, one or possibly more incidents occurred in the early part of the 1900s that could be attributed to the Fouke Monster.

Sources: *Victoria Advocate*, Lyle Blackburn (personal interviews)

October 1910 - Texarkana

A curious story ran in the *Daily Arkansas Gazette* on October, 5, 1910. It mentions a "strange beast" supposedly loose in the area near Spring Lake Park in Texarkana. This location is approximately twenty miles north of Fouke. The article reads in full:

> **Wild Beast at Large** – *A strange beast, which roars like a lion, is reported to be running at large in the woods north of Spring Lake Park near Texarkana. The animal is said to have killed several pigs on the McAllister place and several dogs near New Town. The roars of the strange beast have so frightened the people of that locality that they are afraid to leave their homes after dark and windows and doors are kept securely barred.*

Since the article doesn't provide a description of the creature, it's impossible to know whether it looked anything like an upright ape or "wild man." A lion's roar does not seem very ape-like; however, the Fouke Monster has been said to growl and howl at high volume. It would also be accused of killing pigs in later incidents, so this article does leave one wondering.

Source: *Daily Arkansas Gazette*

1916 - Wright Patman Lake

Another possible early sighting occurred around 1916, approximately nineteen miles west of Fouke near Wright Patman Lake in Texas. While it may seem like a considerable distance, it's worth noting the incident took place near the origin of the Sulphur River, which is part of the larger waterway network that includes Boggy Creek. The story was reported by a retired geologist whose grandparents lived in a place called Knight's Bluff west of Queen City, Texas, and just south of the Sulphur River. (Today there is still a campground on the edge of Wright Patman Lake called Knight's Bluff, but the true Knight's Bluff was covered by water when the lake was created by the U.S. Army Corps of Engineers in 1953.)

According to the geologist, the incident happened on a summer night when his grandmother was eighteen years old. She often told the story, so he and his family knew it well. On the night in question, his grandparents were returning home from town, navigating their mule-drawn wagon across the rough country roads. The moon was high and bright, and visibility was good. As they turned onto the lane leading to their farmhouse, the mules began to act up as if they were spooked by something. Thinking perhaps a snake was in the road, her father peered ahead but saw nothing. A few seconds later they heard a strange noise coming from the east pasture; something like an eerie, high-pitched wail or howl.

The mules heaved as the family struggled to see what had made the noise. After a few moments, they saw a tall figure emerge from a line of shadowy trees adjacent to the field and walk into the moonlight. His grandmother described it as being "tall or taller than a man and covered with long, dark hair." She also noted "it stood absolutely erect and walked slowly toward them like a man... not slouching like an ape."

The creature moved across the field toward the wagon as it continued to howl, all the while motioning angrily at them with its long arms. By now the family was in a state of fear and panic. The father reached for his rifle and fired once in the animal's direction. The shot presumably missed the creature, but the crack of the rifle was enough to send it running back into the woods.

The father managed to get the mules under control and drove the wagon back to the house, where the family promptly jumped out and scrambled for safety. Once inside the house, they barricaded the doors and spent the rest of the night in a state of restless sleep, wondering just what they had seen. The following day and a few days thereafter, the men of the family, along with a few neighbors, scoured the woods near the pasture searching for any signs of blood, fur, or tracks, but nothing was ever found. The family never saw the mysterious creature again.

Source: Charles DeVore

1932 - Fort Lynn

Ace Coker lived with his sister in a house near Fort Lynn, about five miles south of Fouke. According to a story he told to friends and family, he was sitting on the porch one day while his sister was hanging fresh laundry on the clothesline. At some point he got up to go back inside the house. As he opened the screen door, he tilted up his hat, and there standing near the porch was a large, hairy, man-like animal. It had apparently been able to slip up to the porch without making a sound and was now eyeing him curiously. Startled, Coker hurried into the house before looking back again. When he turned around, the thing had already moved out by the fence on their property, and from there it slipped out of sight.

Source: John Attaway

1940s

1943 - Fouke

A serviceman by the name of Haskell Vernon Sowell saw what he described as a "wild man" run across the road while driving a military munitions truck through Fouke. He said the thing bounded over the road in a few long strides and quickly disappeared into the woods. According to Sowell, he had no previous knowledge of the alleged creature.

Source: Lyle Blackburn (interview with a family member)

1946 - Fouke

In 1946, Miller County resident Leslie Greer was campaigning for a local government office when he heard a strange story. According to Greer in a 1971 *Texarkana Gazette* article:

> *I was campaigning for tax assessor and stopped to talk to a lady sitting on her front porch. She lived about halfway between Fouke and the Below Bridge. She told me that she saw some kind of animal go down in the field in a low, bushy place. She said it looked kind of like a man, and walked like a man, but she didn't think it was a man.*

Greer didn't give the story much thought at the time. It was only later, in 1971, when a rash of bizarre sightings were reported around Boggy Creek, did he realize the significance of what the woman had told him.

FOUKE FACTS: Leslie Greer later served as Miller County Sheriff from 1967 to 1974.

Source: *Texarkana Gazette*

1950s

A number of encounters occurred in the mid to late 1950s. The date of some of the incidents are an estimation, but by all accounts the creature sightings seemed to be increasing during this time period. Because many of these sightings took place in Jonesville—a small community located along the Sulphur River south of Fouke—the creature was originally known as the "Jonesville Monster."

1954 - Fouke

Around 1954, a woman and her two children who lived in an isolated farmhouse about two miles from town saw a large, hairy creature in their field. The woman promptly sent her son to fetch the landlord, but this was over two miles away and the boy had to get there on foot. By the time the landlord came to investigate the following morning, the strange visitor was gone.

Source: *Texarkana Gazette*

1955 - Fouke

According to prominent Fouke resident Willie Smith, he saw the creature on two occasions near his home in 1955. The first time, the creature was lurking along Boggy Creek, which ran behind Smith's home. After he determined it was not a man, he shot at it "15 times with an Army rifle." Smith must not have been a very good marksman, since the creature was able to escape unharmed into the woods.

Despite the display of brazen gunfire, Smith said the creature returned a short time later, this time "throwing chunks" at his dog. Once again Smith grabbed his rifle and attempted to shoot the thing, but again he missed, and the creature ran into the woods.

FOUKE FACTS: Willie Smith became one of the central figures in the Fouke Monster case when it exploded in the press in 1971. Not only had Smith reportedly laid eyes on the creature, but mysterious footprints were found in a soybean field he owned during the summer of 1971. Smith also owned a gas station in Fouke and was always willing to speak to reporters who came to town looking for information during the monster's media sensation of the 1970s. Smith also appeared as himself in *The Legend of Boggy Creek* movie.

Source: *Victoria Advocate*

1955 - Jonesville at Sulphur River

In about 1955, James Crabtree reportedly saw a large, gorilla-like creature along the banks of the Sulphur River near Jonesville about five miles south of Fouke. According to Crabtree's great niece, Syble Attaway, James was floating down the river checking his trot lines when he saw the thing sitting on the muddy bank. It appeared to be washing its feet in the water. Crabtree tried to ease up on it in his boat, but it stood up and walked off on two legs. He later told family members he was positive it was not a bear.

FOUKE FACTS: James Crabtree is the uncle of J.E. "Smokey" Crabtree, who would later become a prominent Fouke Monster researcher. According to Smokey and other locals who knew James, he was a very experienced hunter and trapper who would not be likely to mistake typical wildlife for an unknown creature. James's story is featured in *The Legend of Boggy Creek* movie.

Source: Smokey Crabtree with verification from Syble Attaway

1955 - Jonesville

Not long after James Crabtree's sighting (see previous entry), Lee Crabtree and his wife were driving along a country road in Jonesville south of Fouke when something crossed in front of them. It walked like a man yet appeared to have a body covered in hair.

Source: Syble Attaway

The foggy banks of the Sulphur River
(Photo by Lyle Blackburn)

2.

Legendary Encounters

Fouke Monster encounters reported in the 1960s and 1970s have become some of the most widely known of all the incidents. Not only are they dramatic, but many of these were effectively reenacted in *The Legend of Boggy Creek* movie.

The incidents that occurred in the 1960s were attributed to a creature the locals were calling the "Jonesville Monster." When a new rash of incidents made headlines in 1971, the *Texarkana Gazette* newspaper dubbed the creature the "Fouke Monster." Since this was in newsprint, it became the creature's primary name. After the release of *The Legend of Boggy Creek*, the Fouke Monster was also referred to as the "Boggy Creek Monster."

1960s

1964 - Jonesville

An especially chilling account came from Mary Beth Searcy who lived in the area of Jonesville near the Sulphur River south of Fouke. Mary Beth, a teenager at the time, was spending a night at home with her mother, older sister, and baby niece, while her brother and father were spending the night elsewhere. When the other women went to bed early with the baby, Mary Beth continued doing her schoolwork. As the spring air cooled with the deepening night, Mary Beth's sister asked her to cover the bedroom window to prevent the baby from becoming ill. Mary Beth grabbed a blanket and approached the window. As she was covering it, she glanced into the yard, which was bathed in enough sparse moonlight to see the immediate area between the house and the outlying trees. She was shocked to see a large, hairy creature emerging from the woods. It walked on two legs as though it were human. She screamed and ran from the window as the other two women bolted awake. They spent the rest of the night in sleepless terror.

FOUKE FACTS: Mary Beth's sighting was reenacted as a feature scene in *The Legend of Boggy Creek* movie. The scene was filmed at the actual Searcy home where Mary Beth saw the creature. The role of Mary Beth was played by Texarkana resident, Judy Haltom, while the role of Mary Beth's older sister was played by Mary Beth herself. The experience of seeing the creature haunted Mary Beth the rest of her life. She passed away on December 2, 2019.

Sources: Mary Beth Searcy, Smokey Crabtree

1965 - Jonesville

Fred Crabtree said he was hunting in the dense backwoods near Jonesville south of Fouke when he noticed a dark, shadowy creature as it stood among the thick trees. He tried to move closer for a better look, but before he could, the thing slipped out of sight. He said he could have shot it, but it was impossible to tell if it was truly an animal or if it was some kind of wild man. He thought it was best not to gamble.

FOUKE FACTS: This sighting took place a few months prior to Lynn Crabtree's encounter with what is presumably the same creature or another of its kind. (See next entry.) Fred's incident was also dramatized in *The Legend of Boggy Creek*.

Source: Smokey Crabtree

1965 - Jonesville at Crabtree Lake

One evening in 1965[i], James Lynn Crabtree (who went by his middle name, Lynn) was hunting squirrels by himself in the dense woods of the Sulphur River Bottoms behind Crabtree Lake. (The lake was created by his father, Smokey, and was on their large tract of land in Jonesville.) As the sun began to set, Lynn was sitting under a tall acorn tree waiting for squirrels. Suddenly he heard the sound of horses running down a nearby logging trail. They eventually splashed into waters of the lake, which was about seventy-five yards away. The horses belonged to one of the neighbors and often ran wild through the woods, so this was nothing out of the ordinary. Lynn figured they were seeking relief from flies and other insects by running into the water.

About the time the horses hit the water, a dog began bellowing in pain. The sound was coming from the same location near the lake. Lynn thought it might be one of their own dogs, perhaps hung up in a fence, so he got up and began to head in that direction. He was about halfway to the lake when the dog's bellow changed to some kind of deep grunt or groan. Lynn had never heard anything like it so he stopped a moment to listen. As he focused on the noise, he realized it was not coming from the dog, but instead from some kind of big animal he had never heard before. It was completely unnerving.

Lynn walked forward to a clearing where he could get a better look. As soon as he cleared the trees and the lake was in view, he saw some kind of hairy animal standing near the water with its back to him no more than thirty feet away. The thing was watching the horses and moving in such a way that gave Lynn the impression it was angry.

The horrified hunter stood silent as he observed the creature,

---

i   The year of Lynn Crabtree's encounter has been noted as 1963 in various sources, but his father, Smokey, implicitly cites the year 1965 in his book, *Smokey and the Fouke Monster*.

which appeared to be

some type of "hairy man or gorilla type beast with very long arms." Lynn realized *it* had been the reason the horses fled for the safety of the lake.

The beast, which was moving its head and shoulders in an agitated manner, suddenly turned and looked directly at Lynn. The boy, who was a fearless youth, trembled at the sight of the disturbing thing. Its face was obscured by hair with "only a dark brown nose showing, flat and close to his face."

Thinking it must surely be a man, Lynn raised his gun in an attempt to frighten him off. He only had squirrel shot in his rifle, but it would be threatening enough. The bizarre manimal paid no heed to the firearm and started walking toward the boy. Lynn shouted a warning before he fired off a round. He aimed for the head, but the beast seemed totally unaffected as it continued to advance. Lynn shot off two more rounds before finally fleeing in panic. When he reached his house, he frantically told his mother and father what he had seen.

FOUKE FACTS: This incident is what drew Smokey Crabtree and his family into the midst of the Fouke Monster case. Smokey would later become an important part of the filming of *The Legend of Boggy Creek*, while several of his family's stories would be reenacted in it. From the night of Lynn's sighting forward, Smokey was committed to finding proof of the Fouke Monster, not only to satisfy his own curiosity but to substantiate Lynn's story, for which Lynn suffered ridicule at school and other places. Lynn passed away on April 20, 2011. Julius Elmo "Smokey" Crabtree passed away on January 16, 2016.

Source: Smokey Crabtree

1965 - Jonesville

Less than one month after Lynn Crabtree's encounter (see previous entry), fourteen-year-old Jonesville resident, Kenneth Dyas, said he saw a similar hairy creature while deer hunting. Dyas fired at the creature, then fled out of the woods as fast as he could.

Source: Smokey Crabtree

1965 - Jonesville at Sulphur River

Sometime after Lynn and Kenneth reported their sightings, Phyllis Brown was deer hunting southwest of Fouke near the Sulphur River when she heard dogs running what she thought was a deer. She turned and looked up the clear-cut of a pipeline and noticed what she thought was a "black guy" running toward her. The figure was distant at first, but as it got closer she realized it was not a person but something covered in hair running upright like a man. The thing was moving in a northwesterly direction behind her, and when it passed by, she got a good look at it. She said it was not something she had ever seen before.

Source: Frank McFerrin (Miller County Historical Museum)

1965 - Jonesville Area

During the sightings outbreak of the mid-1960s, Smokey Crabtree and others attempted to hunt down the creature. At one point, nearly twenty locals armed with guns, horses, and tracking dogs scouted the area but were unable to find it. One member of the search party, Jimmy Cornett, was riding his horse through the bottoms when some kind of large animal passed nearby, causing his horse to throw him. He could not say whether the animal he saw was a bear, a "gorilla," or something else.

Source: Smokey Crabtree

1966 - Fouke

While en route to pick up children early one morning, a Fouke school bus driver reported seeing the alleged creature cross the road.

Source: Smokey Crabtree

1966/1967 - Jonesville at Crabtree Lake

For a few years after Lynn Crabtree's encounter, his father Smokey Crabtree said the creature would periodically stalk around their home. According to Smokey in his book, *Smokey and the Fouke Monster*:

> *The thing came up to our house several times, at night only. He would scream out a few times and run the dogs away from home for a few days, but they would always come back. The cattle would stampede and run through the woods from him. We would get out there with guns and lights. I was never sure enough of what I saw to shoot.*

Source: Smokey Crabtree

1967 - Fouke

Around 1967, Charlie Walraven was driving toward his home on County Road 9 late one evening. As his old Ford sedan coughed its way along the lonely stretch of rural road, a man-like creature darted out in front of him. It was only visible for a few seconds before it disappeared into the thick trees on the opposite side of the road. Walraven said it was definitely running on two legs and looked to be covered in hair.

Source: Frank McFerrin (Miller County Historical Museum)

Spring 1967 - Fouke at Sulphur River

In the spring of 1967, musician Carl Finch and his cousin were driving north on the lonely stretch of Highway 71 south of Fouke near the Sulphur River. Earlier that evening, he and his band at the time had performed at a "Battle of the Bands" in Shreveport, Louisiana. After the show, he and his cousin were making the late-night drive from Shreveport back to Texarkana—where he was living at the time—in her Volkswagen Beetle. As they traveled along 71, they noticed an upright figure in the headlights running alongside the road in front of them. It was traveling in the same direction as their car, and as they got closer, they could see it was running at a fairly rapid pace. Finch's first impression was it must be "a guy in a brown coat." That seemed rather odd, however, because this was a very dangerous and unlikely place for a man to be out jogging late at night. Besides, the weather at the time did not warrant a heavy coat, especially if one intended to work up a sweat.

As they closed the gap, it became increasingly apparent there was something bizarre about the late-night runner. Finch could see it had really long arms and fur, and it was running swiftly with a gait that did not seem human. The creature did not react to the car's presence. It simply kept on running as they sped by.

Once they had passed the figure, the headlights no longer provided illumination, so it was impossible to get a good look at the face. And they were too scared to stop. Once they passed the creature—or whatever it was—it simply faded into blackness...and eventually into memory.

It wasn't until the mid-1970s, when Finch caught a showing of *The Legend of Boggy Creek*, did he recall their sighting. Seeing the story of the Fouke Monster on the big screen and learning about its connection to the lonely stretch of Highway 71 gave him pause. Was it the Fouke Monster he and his cousin had seen years before? Finch believes it is a definite possibility.

FOUKE FACTS: Carl Finch would later form the popular polka/rock band, Brave Combo, from Denton, Texas. Founded in 1979, the band has gone on to enjoy a wide following and legendary status with a slew of honors including two Grammy awards, an appearance on *The Simpsons* cartoon, and a cameo in the 1995 feature film, *Late Bloomers*, among other achievements.

His report is significant to the Jonesville-era monster, since Finch's sighting seemed to corroborate what the locals were also reporting. Finch and his cousin did not live in Jonesville or Fouke, and at the time they had no knowledge of what had been going on there with the "monster sightings." Finch told me he hadn't heard of the Fouke Monster or even Bigfoot at the time. If the residents of Jonesville had been caught up in some mass hallucination or hoax, Finch was certainly not a part. Yet the creature he describes seeing that night matches very closely with what they have described.

Source: Lyle Blackburn (personal interview)

Mid to Late 1960s - Mercer Bayou

A man was hunting in the flooded woods of Mercer Bayou when he saw a seven-foot-tall, hairy, man-like animal. He tried to approach it, but the creature disappeared into the thick underbrush.

Source: Lyle Blackburn

The flooded woods of Mercer Bayou
(Photo by Lyle Blackburn)

1968 - Jonesville

Sometime around 1968, the creature was seen on two separate occasions a few miles south of Fouke as it searched for food around the home of Louise Harvin. The first encounter occurred at sunrise one morning as Ms. Harvin prepared for work. She heard a ruckus in her hog pen, so she went outside to check on her animals. When she headed across the yard toward the pen, she was startled to see a large, hair-covered animal standing on two legs inside the fence eating from a pile of scraps that had been left out the night before. She said the animal had long, reddish hair that covered its body, while its face was a darker shade of brown with a large, flat nose. Food scraps hung from its mouth and clung to the fur of its chest and hands. When it saw the woman, the creature immediately stopped eating. Within seconds, it jumped the fence and disappeared into the woods. Startled, but not overly frightened by the strange beast, Ms. Harvin continued on to work, although at the time she told no one what she had seen.

The creature made a second visit a short time later. On this occasion, Ms. Harvin was stepping out onto the porch early one morning when she surprised the animal. It was licking remnants of food from an old hubcap that was being used as a dog bowl. As before, the creature paused and looked at her. Ms. Harvin noted the creature's scraggly hair and its ability to stand on two legs. She could also see it had rather long canine teeth, which resembled those of "a baboon, although the face was much more flat like that of a gorilla." After a few seconds, the animal bounded off into the woods, never to be seen by Ms. Harvin again.

FOUKE FACTS: Her son Mackey, who was off serving in the war at the time, did not hear of his mother's encounters until a few years later when he returned. He was already familiar with the sighting by his friend Lynn Crabtree and the incident at the Searcy house, so he was not completely surprised his mother had also seen the creature. Given the creature's flat, brown nose and overall hairy body, he feels quite certain his mother had been surprised by the same creature, or one of its kind, that Lynn had seen. Mackey did not feel his mother would have any reason to make up such a wild tale.

Source: Lyle Blackburn (interview with witness's son)

November 1968 - Sulphur River

In November or December of 1968, a father and his thirteen-year-old son decided to go duck hunting in the Sulphur River Wildlife Management Area west of Fouke. They towed their boat to the Sulphur River's new public entry ramp east of Long Slough (which had just been constructed at the time) and launched it into the water. After hunting all morning, they motored the boat back to the ramp and pulled it from the water. It was around noon by this time, so they prepared a lunch and stood in front of their truck while they ate and talked. It was a pleasant, clear day, and they enjoyed the peaceful respite.

While they were eating, an awful smell began to fill the air. They looked around trying to figure out the source of the stench, but they saw nothing. They tried to resume their lunch, but the smell only got worse. Soon, they noticed a "dark, man-like figure" walking across the roadway that led to the boat ramp. The road itself was approximately twenty-five feet wide and there were about thirty feet of cleared timber on either side, making it a considerable gap. At this point, the figure was fairly far away, perhaps two hundred yards, but even then it appeared to be larger and more muscular than an average man – if it were even a man at all.

The father and son observed the thing as it crossed the clearing with "very long and deliberate strides" of at least eight feet and headed toward the river at fairly quick pace. They said it moved in a rather peculiar way with its forearms parallel to the ground, as if it were carrying something. The witnesses could not see what it was carrying (if anything); however, since it had long hair covering its midsection, a small animal carcass or an offspring could easily have been obscured.

The hunters continued to watch in amazement as they tried to figure out just what the thing was. It appeared to be over eight feet tall and was covered in "shaggy and patchy hair." The hair was primarily a "rusty-red" in color but was streaked in black. Its body was very thick and muscular with virtually no neck. Because of this and the amount of hair, they could not get a good look at the face before it disappeared into the thick woods.

The creature never looked in their direction or acknowledged their presence in any way, so the hunters assumed it had not seen them. However, just to be safe, the father retrieved his shotgun from the cab of their truck and loaded it. He watched the woods with a close eye as he and his son ate the rest of their lunch. The once pleasant day had taken a chilling turn. Even the birds, which had been singing and flitting about prior to the creature's appearance, were now still and silent. It was an incident they would never forget.

Source: Tal H. Branco

1969 - Jonesville

Yet another sighting of the mystery beast occurred in 1969, although the details of this one are somewhat thin. According to retired Sheriff H.L. Phillips, two coon hunters were hunting south of Fouke when they proceeded down into a draw. When they reached the bottom, they turned and noticed something standing behind them. It was a large, upright creature on two legs covered with bushy hair. Just how the men reacted is not known, but presumably they either retreated up the draw, or the creature slipped away into the woods before they could get a better look.

FOUKE FACTS: H.L. Phillips served in Miller County law enforcement from 1969 until he retired in 2006. He was instrumental in fielding a number of Fouke Monster reports, which he took seriously.

Source: H.L. Phillips

December 1969 - Fouke

John Copeland and his family were driving on Highway 71 north of Fouke at night when they spotted what they thought was a man in a fur coat walking toward them on the opposite side of the road. It was cold and close to Christmas, so they decided to slow down and offer him a ride. When they got closer, they realized it was not a man in a coat, but instead some kind of thing covered in hair. As they approached with the bright lights on, the thing stopped and raised its arm to shield its eyes from the light.

They could see its arm was thick and muscular, and its body was covered in brown, shaggy hair with longer hair over its face. Its legs appeared to be caked in mud from the knees down as if it had just come from the river bottoms or a muddy creek. Copeland was afraid the thing would endanger his family, so he quickly sped off.

FOUKE FACTS: This location would have been close to the Ford property where the creature would make huge headlines in 1971. (See entry *April 28 through May 2, 1971.*)

Source: *Sasquatch Chronicles*

Early 1970s

The incidents reported in the early 1970s resulted in a frenzy of press coverage and directly inspired Charles B. Pierce to make *The Legend of Boggy Creek*. Due to a heightened awareness created by the press in 1971, that particular year would see a record number of Fouke Monster reports.

Around 1970 - Fouke

1) A man and his son saw the alleged creature running on two legs across their field. It appeared to be wounded.

Source: As told to Charles B. Pierce

2) A local farmer told Charles Pierce he had gone out to milk his cows one morning when he surprised the creature. He told Pierce: "It was standing there, looking at me. He stepped out, and the back barn door was open, and the light was at his back. He twisted his head and looked at me very curiously, backed up a couple of steps, and then started walking off across my back pasture toward the woods. The hair drooped off his shoulders, off his arms, and he didn't have any clothes on. The hair completely covered his body."

Source: *Fangoria* magazine #165, interview with Charles B. Pierce

April 28 through May 2, 1971 - Fouke

During the last week of April in 1971, two families moved to a small rental home located at the north end of Fouke on Highway 71. The families were Don and Patricia Ford and their four children and Charles and Elizabeth Taylor, who did not have any children. The men had come to the area for work and were eager to settle into their new home. But their experience there would be far from settling.

On the night of Wednesday, April 28, they heard something moving around outside the home. They could hear the sound of its footsteps creaking along the old boards of the porch. The house was a simple, frame structure with a covered porch on the front side and woods surrounding the perimeter. The Fords and Taylors were not sure who or what was "fooling around the house," but it was enough to send them fleeing to the closest neighbor's home with all the children in tow. After they calmed down, the couples returned to the house, and nothing further happened that night.

Two days later, on Friday May 1, Don's younger brother, Bobby Ford, and a friend, Corky Hill, arrived at the home. They planned to stay the weekend and do some fishing at a nearby creek. After visiting with Don, Patricia, and the Taylors, Bobby and Corky headed to the creek with their fishing poles. When they arrived, they immediately found a strange-looking footprint pressed into the mud along the bank. It was long and human-like, yet only had three toes. The creepy-looking track, along with the rather ominous atmosphere of the woods, made them so nervous they abandoned the idea of fishing and headed straight back to the house.

Later that night, the mysterious visitor returned. Again, the residents could hear it walking around on the porch. According to Bobby, the thing later tried to "break into" the home, which only heightened the sense of fear growing in the household. This time they stayed inside until whatever it was eventually left.

The following night, Saturday May 2, Bobby was using the bathroom when the thing suddenly appeared at the window. He immediately abandoned his business and ran into the living room. Elizabeth Taylor[ii] was sitting on the couch in the living room when she saw the curtain moving in an open window. Suddenly a hairy, clawed hand came through the opening. Its eyes flashed briefly, reflecting red in the glow of the interior light.

"At first I thought it was a bear's paw but it didn't look like that," Mrs. Taylor told a reporter from the *Texarkana Gazette*. "It had heavy hair all over it and it had claws and I could see its eyes. They looked like coals of fire…real red. It didn't make any noise. Except you could hear it breathing."

By then Bobby was sitting in a chair holding a butcher's knife. When the hand came through the window, he grabbed Elizabeth and threw her on the floor in an effort to protect her. However, the thing did not try to gain entrance through the window.

When Don and Charles became aware of the situation, they grabbed a flashlight and a shotgun (which they had previously borrowed from Fouke Constable Ernest Walraven) and rushed out the front door. Bobby followed close behind. The three men saw a "large, hairy animal" run toward the back of the house. They estimated it was "about seven feet tall and about three feet wide across the chest." It was running upright on two legs. One of them shot at it several times, but apparently missed. "At that point, everyone in the house saw it move rapidly into the field next to the house and then it was gone," they later told reporters.

Don, Charles, and Bobby went back inside the house and placed a call to Constable Walraven. Concerned for their safety, Walraven got into his car and drove to the scene. The constable arrived at 12:35 a.m. and spent approximately one hour searching

---

ii In the primary article published by the *Texarkana Gazette* on May 3, 1971, Elizabeth Taylor is misidentified as "Elizabeth Ford." Patricia Ford corrected this error in a letter she sent to the *Texarkana Gazette* in September 1972.

the fields and woods surround the house. He found no evidence of the intruder, but he decided to leave another shotgun and a powerful flashlight just in case it returned. He then bid the Fords good night and drove off.

The actual house the Fords were renting in the spring of 1971. (Photo courtesy of the Miller County Historical Society)

Armed with two shotguns and two flashlights, Don, Charles, and Bobby now stood guard on the porch while the women, children, and Corky Hill remained inside. It wasn't long until the thing returned, this time "kicking in the back door" as it tried to get inside. The men responded quickly, illuminating it with a flashlight while firing at it with the shotguns. The thing fled toward the woods, again running on two legs.

"We shot again and thought we saw it fall," Don Ford said. "Bobby, Charles and myself started walking to where we saw it fall."

As the three men walked toward the woods to look for the body, they heard the women in the house begin screaming. Bobby turned and headed back to check on them while Don and Charles continued ahead. As Bobby was climbing the steps to the elevated porch, something leapt from the shadows and grabbed him. According to Bobby:

> *I was walking the rungs of a ladder to get up on the porch when the thing grabbed me. I felt a hairy arm come over my shoulder and the next thing I knew we were on the ground. The only thing I could think about was to get out of there. The thing was breathing real hard and his eyes were about the size of a half dollar and real red. I finally broke away and ran around the house and through the front door. I don't know where he [it] went."*

When Don and Charles heard Bobby shouting, they turned and ran toward the porch. By the time they got there, however, the red-eyed creature had disappeared into the woods again, and Bobby was already in the house. He hadn't completely broken through the front door, but his arm had gone through the glass. Patricia got him inside and tried to help. Bobby was in total shock, and as Patricia put it, "out of his head." He was also scratched up from the attack. The Fords put Bobby into the car and headed for Constable Walraven's house. According to Patricia:

> *We did go back to the constable's house when Bobby was in shock. Bobby kept coming to on the way to the hospital. He was screaming and trying to kick out the car windows so Don would knock him back every time he came to. We had no police escort. We escorted ourselves to St. Michael's Hospital by blowing the car horn and running every red light from Fouke to St. Michaels.*

*It seemed to us that the thing was after our dog because
every room our dog went into was where the thing tried
to get in next.*

Walraven sent them off to the hospital in Texarkana, then returned to the Ford house and remained there until 5:00 a.m. The
creature—or whatever it was—did not return.

At the hospital, Bobby was treated for injuries and tested for
the presence of alcohol in his blood at the request of Walraven.
The doctors determined Bobby had not been drinking.

After sunrise, more Miller County police officials arrived at the
Ford house—including then deputy H.L. Phillips. During the investigation, the lawmen found pieces of metal around the bottom
of the house that had been "ripped away." They also noted window
damage and scratches on the front porch. In the soil around the
house, they discovered curious tracks, which may have been left
by the creature. Whatever it was appeared to have only three toes.

Reporters also showed up at the scene. One of these was Dave
Hall, news director for Texarkana's KTFS radio station. He had
been tipped off by one of the doctors at St. Michaels. Hall in turn
called his friend Jim Powell, a journalist at the *Texarkana Gazette*,
and suggested they drive to the home to check it out. When the
two reporters arrived, they found the Fords in a state of frenzy.
They were packing their belongings into a U-Haul in a tremendous hurry. Powell and Hall proceeded to search the immediate
area for evidence along with the police. There was a freshly plowed
field behind the house, so the men looked for tracks where the
Fords said they had seen glowing eyes.

"We went into the area behind the house and saw unusual
footprints, and small saplings broken off," Hall told me in an interview. "We never saw any blood, although the people said they
fired several shots and thought they hit it."

The Ford house was slowly becoming the scene of a mob as
onlookers were beginning to gather and even taking it upon them-

selves to join the search for the "monster." However, they quickly trampled any potential track evidence, which was probably minimal anyway since it had rained earlier that morning.

The authorities theorized the intruder might have been a panther (i.e., a cougar), since there was evidence something may have been living under the house. Faint footprints found near the porch seemed to be those of a panther. Even Don Ford later suggested it might have been a wildcat, although this was in stark contrast to the family's original assessment. (Perhaps Don was trying to downplay the story in an attempt to alleviate the frenzy of people now invading their privacy.) Rumors also circulated that the perpetrator could have been a horse. Several sources agreed that an old horse had been seen lumbering around the area of Highway 71 where the house was located. It often trampled through gardens and approached houses at night. However, no hoof prints were found anywhere near the scene, not to mention at least five adults had all seen something—which they described as being tall, hairy, and running on two legs—fleeing toward the woods. (And horses certainly do not have hairy hands and red eyes.) Other vague rumors suggested it was locals or even police officials perpetrating a hoax in an attempt to get the families to leave Fouke. Deputy H.L. Phillips—who later became sheriff—dismissed the rumor as unfounded. (I spoke to him at length about this case.)

The Ford and Taylor families promptly moved from the home and never returned to Fouke.

FOUKE FACTS: The incidents that occurred at the "Ford House" were the first to be covered by the *Texarkana Gazette* newspaper in an article dated May 3, 1971. Though sightings of a similarly described creature had occurred in the area prior to this time, it was this article that signaled the beginning of the Fouke Monster's media exposure. Jim Powell, the journalist who wrote the article, was the person responsible for giving the creature its name as the "Fouke Monster." The Fords' ordeal has also become the most famous and sensational of the Fouke Monster incidents in part because it was the basis for the climactic segment of *The Legend of Boggy Creek* movie.

Sources: *Texarkana Gazette*, letter from Patricia Ford to the *Texarkana Gazette*, *The Camden News*, Lyle Blackburn (personal interviews)

May 24, 1971 - Fouke at Boggy Creek

On the night of May 24, 1971, Mr. and Mrs. D.C. Woods Jr. and Mrs. R.H. Sedgass (all citizens of Texarkana) were traveling north on Highway 71 when they saw a large animal with "dark long hair" run upright across the road in front of their car and disappear into the darkness beyond. They were near the location where Boggy Creek crosses under the highway.

Mr. Woods thought they were going to collide with the animal, but due to its unusually fast pace, it ran past unharmed. In a highly publicized article in the *Texarkana Gazette* newspaper, the witnesses noted "it was swinging its arms" as it ran and "looked like a giant monkey." The group had recently read about the Ford incident (see previous entry), so they were all aware of the monster at the time and even stated they thought it was just a hoax. But after what they saw on Highway 71, their minds were unequivocally changed. Mrs. Sedgass was quoted as saying: "Some people don't think there is anything to it (the monster), but I do," summing up the feeling shared by the trio.

FOUKE FACTS: The Miller County Sheriff at the time, Leslie Greer, was quoted as saying, "I know those people, and they were very reliable and very truthful. I don't know what they saw, but I do believe they saw something." This article was the first to call the creature the "Fouke Monster."

Source: *Texarkana Gazette*

June 1, 1971 - Fouke (approximate date)

Willie Smith's niece-in-law, Bobbie, claimed to have seen the creature on or around June 1 at the edge of a soybean field behind Smith's home near Boggy Creek. She said the creature stood approximately six feet tall and was covered in hair. She watched it walk through the woods at about 7:30 p.m. in the evening.

Source: *Texarkana Gazette*

June 2, 1971 - Texarkana

On the evening of June 2, law enforcement officials responded to a call from three individuals claiming they had seen a "tall hairy creature with red eyes" near Texarkana. According to one of the witnesses, Gloria Dean Richey, they spotted the creature "squatting" on an embankment across the street from her Oats Street residence after hearing something walk through a wooded area near the road. "We shined a flashlight on the spot and saw the creature," Richey told reporters. "He was real tall and hairy and had real red eyes." When the light hit the creature, the dogs began to bark wildly. At that point the thing started running through the heavy brush "leaping high over the weeds and running faster than a man could."

Mrs. Richey glimpsed the animal once more, approximately twenty-five yards from where it first entered the heavy brush, before it finally disappeared for good. At that point the other witnesses, Junior Goodman and Jerry Smallwood, went to retrieve their guns and call police. When they returned, they followed a trail of trampled weeds and bushes, but could not find any further trace of the creature. Mrs. Richey waited in the house for the men to return. She later told reporters: "I have never seen anything like it. I know it wasn't a cat or a man. I could still hear the dogs acting up and the brush breaking and rattling. I didn't go out again until [Goodman and Smallwood] got back."

The police searched the wooded area around the house shortly after receiving the call but came up empty handed.

Source: *Texarkana Gazette*

June 5, 1971 - Texarkana

On June 5, police received yet another call from a residence at the intersection of Oats and Washington streets. (See previous entry.) This time a child had reported seeing a "monster in the woods across from a group of houses in the area." At the request of the residents, a more thorough search of the area turned up some unidentified tracks at an abandoned fertilizer plant on North Oats Road. (Refer to the *June 6, 1971* entry in **The Evidence** chapter for full details.)

Source: *Texarkana Gazette*

June 13, 1971 - Fouke

A line of mysterious, three-toed footprints was found in a freshly plowed bean field owned by Fouke resident, Willie Smith. They were discovered by farmer, Yother Kennedy, when he dropped by the field that morning to inspect the beans. Refer to the *June 13, 1971* entry in **The Evidence** chapter for full details.

FOUKE FACTS: A curious incident that occurred just prior to the track find was also reported by Kennedy: "Kennedy said he was plowing Wednesday and had stopped to work on his tractor when he heard strange noises coming from the thick undergrowth near the field. He said he got his rifle and plowed the rest of the day with it close by. Then Sunday he returned to the field to see how his beans were doing and found the tracks."

Sources: *Texarkana Gazette*

*Miller County Constable Paul Jewell inspects tracks
found at a fertilizer plant on June 6, 1971
(Photo courtesy of the Texarkana Gazette)*

June 16, 1971 - Fouke

In the early morning hours of June 16, Fouke residents Al Williams and A. L. Tipton observed an ape-like animal "slouch" across a gravel road in front of their car. The road ran two miles south of Fouke, only a quarter mile from Smith's soybean field (see previous entry). They were close enough to see that the creature was either a "small ape or large monkey." Tipton stated that "it appeared to be about three or four feet tall as it crouched over and walked across the road." Although the height estimation seemed at odds with the seven-foot range, it reinforced the theory that some kind of ape-like creature may be living in the area. And if it was a real animal, then it likely had offspring, which could explain this creature's smaller stature. The men reported the sighting to Sheriff Leslie Greer.

Source: *Texarkana Gazette*

Late June, 1971 - Fouke

In late June of 1971, two men from Kansas stopped into town to ask about what kind of wild animals were thought to inhabit the area. Several of the Fouke locals figured the two men were joking about "the monster" and immediately laughed it off. But when the locals began to speak of their would-be beast, the men were shocked. They claimed to have no knowledge of the recent incidents. They were only concerned because they had seen some kind of peculiar-looking, two-legged animal standing by the side of the road. After hearing the story of the Fouke Monster, the visitors promptly left the area.

Source: *Texarkana Gazette*

Late June, 1971 - Fouke

In a *Texarkana Gazette* news article, Sheriff Leslie Greer stated that a group of several women and children, who had traveled to the area to look at the tracks in the soybean field, reported seeing an ape-like creature nearby.

Source: *Texarkana Gazette*

Fall 1971 - Mercer Bayou

In the fall of 1971, Butch Hamilton and his parents drove to Mercer Bayou, west of Fouke, for a day of boating. When they pulled into Mercer's public boat ramp, Butch noticed a medium-sized camper parked at the north end of the circular parking area near the woods. The camper looked well-used and had streams of rust running down its dirty, white exterior. A Suburban-type vehicle was parked in front of it, but no occupants could be seen.

Butch's father made a U-turn and backed the boat trailer down to the water. When he came to a stop, Butch and his mother jumped out of their truck. He loved to explore the area around the ramp, so he wasted no time dragging his mother toward the trees to look for animal tracks or other interesting things.

Butch's father took to the task of preparing their boat. It was a ruddy green craft with a motor that did not always live up to its expectations. This time it must have needed more coaxing, being that his father grabbed a toolbox from the back of their truck.

While his father worked on the boat, Butch and his mother collected pull-can tabs from the dirt and poked around in the leaves. He wouldn't mind if the old boat motor never started; he could have plenty of fun right there. Besides, the bayou got a little creepy at night. He knew his mother and father would not put him in danger, but still there was something about the moss and groaning bullfrogs that could make a ten-year-old boy feel uneasy out on the dark water.

Butch and his mother continued to walk around the perimeter of the parking area. At one point he thought he could see movement inside the white camper, but so far no one had emerged. His mother was just about to go check on his father, when something howled from the woods north of the camper. At first he thought it might be a bird, but after hearing it a second time, he could tell it was definitely an animal noise. It sounded like a coarse, moaning howl.

Butch's mother heard the sound, too, and tilted her head upward as if listening intently. She then attempted to call back by imitating the sound as closely as she could. Butch was impressed at how close she came. His mother was nearly full-blooded Native American and always took pride in her connection to animals and nature. This was the type of thing she really enjoyed.

After a few moments the animal made its strange cry again, this time ending the howl with something of a scream. Was it responding to his mother? She cupped her hand to her mouth and called back. The sound echoed into the woods, which were just beginning to fill with late afternoon shadows. This time the animal howled back immediately, sounding much closer.

As his mother made a third response, the door of the white camper opened. Butch saw one man, then two more emerge and step down onto the parking lot. They looked at him and his mother briefly, then turned toward the woods. One of them held a shotgun.

Butch and his mother watched with apprehension as the three men made their way around the camper to get a better look into the trees. As they rounded the corner, Butch could hear something approaching. It sounded like a man walking through the leaves. Butch felt a chill run up his back. What started out as exciting was starting to get weird.

The men said nothing, which must have made his mother even more nervous. She prompted him to head back toward the truck where his father was still tinkering with the boat, oblivious to what was happening at the other end of the drive. When Butch got halfway to the truck, he turned and looked back toward the woods. At that point he saw a hairy, reddish-brown creature walk into view. It stood perhaps seven to eight feet tall, but hunched slightly as it stopped and looked at the men. It appeared to be studying them from the safety of the trees.

Butch bolted for the truck and jumped inside. His mother, not having seen the creature, was walking toward the water where his father was working. Butch continued to observe the creature from the car. It slowly moved closer, stepping up onto an old log, but still keeping a safe distance from the men who remained by the camper. The man with the shotgun gripped it with both hands, but did not raise it.

Through the open window of the cab, Butch could hear his mother saying something to his father, but otherwise the whole scene was suspended in a strange, surreal silence. He watched for what seemed like several minutes as the creature held its wary position among the trees. The men, like Butch, merely observed in awe, as if they couldn't figure out what course of action to take. He glanced at his parents, who were still standing near the boat. His father seemed angry and was having a heated conversation with his mother.

Butch turned his attention back to the creature, which now stepped over the log. For a moment he wondered if it was going to run out and attack the men, but the thought was shattered when he heard the boat motor roar to life. At that point the creature turned and darted into the trees out of sight.

Butch backed away from the window and scrambled out of the cab. As he ran toward his mother, he prayed the boat motor would just sputter out and quit. He did not want to take a ride into the bayou that night. Whatever was living in those woods, he did not want to see again.

Source: Lyle Blackburn (personal interview)

1972 to 1979

Summer 1972 - Fouke

In the summer of 1972, a Fouke resident was driving along one of the backroads near his home when a hairy creature walked into the road. It looked briefly toward his vehicle before it continued into the thick brush beside the road. The witness did not get a good look at the face, but it clearly walked on two legs and was covered in hair. It was also rather short in stature.

Source: Jose' Porfirio Gonzales

May or June 1973 - Jonesville

On a Sunday afternoon in the early summer of 1973, two young teens, Reba Jones and Karen Crabtree, were riding in the back of a pickup truck along one of the county roads in Jonesville. They were sitting on a spare tire and looking behind the truck when a huge, hairy, man-like animal walked into the road where the vehicle had just passed. It stepped to the middle of the road with a long stride and stopped.

"I can see it just as clear as day as I did then," Jones told me as we spoke one afternoon in Fouke. "It stepped out and just looked at us."

The creature was immense and completely covered in hair. Jones estimated its height to be over seven feet tall and a body width at least three times that of a human. It stood completely upright on two legs, which accentuated the length of its arms.

"It wasn't hunched over; it was standing straight up," she recalled. "And what really impressed me was its arms. They were really long."

The startled girls observed the creature for a few seconds before it walked into some heavy brush on the other side of the road and disappeared from sight. They began banging on the cab of truck, trying to get the driver to stop so they could go back to look for it. The adults in the cab, however, just laughed it off and continued driving.

Since they were teenagers, no one tended to believe their story. It was always dismissed as being the product of a "wild imagination." But Reba is adamant about what she and Karen saw that day. "That was no imagination," she affirmed.

FOUKE FACTS: Karen Davis Crabtree would later paint a mural of the creature on the outside of the Monster Mart convenience store in Fouke. Sadly, she was killed in an automobile accident in 2009.

Source: Lyle Blackburn (personal interview)

November 25, 1973 - Fouke

On the morning of November 25, 1973, Orville Scoggins observed a black-haired, four-foot tall creature creep across his bean field. According to Scoggins, he was outside his home when he heard an odd noise. When he looked up, he could see the strange animal about one hundred yards away, walking slowly in an eastward direction. The animal remained upright on two feet the entire time. Scoggins estimated its weight to be around eighty to ninety pounds.

After the sighting, Scoggins jumped in his pickup and raced to the Fouke Café, where he found Constable Red Walraven. Upon hearing the story, Walraven and two other men went back to Scoggins's farm, which was located four miles from Fouke's main strip. Upon inspecting the area where the creature had been sighted, they found a line of tracks in the soil. The tracks measured five and a half inches in diameter and were spaced forty inches apart. The men followed the tracks for nearly an eighth of a mile before the trail finally disappeared into the woods. They conducted a thorough search of the area, but did not locate the animal.

FOUKE FACTS: Scoggins was not confident he had seen

the Fouke Monster, but he was positive he had seen something unusual. Scoggins had always been known as a die-hard monster skeptic, but after this incident, he changed his mind saying, "Something stalks the woods near Fouke."

Source: *Texarkana Gazette*

Officers gird for Fouke 'monster hunt'

Monster hunting near Fouke, Ark. may prove to be a popular pasttime this weekend but persons doing the hunting better leave guns and liquor at home, advises Miller County Sheriff L.B. (Leslie) Greer.

Greer said Thursday in response to reports of teenagers planning a monster hunt Friday night that deputies and other law enforcement officers will be checking cars for guns and liquor in the area where the "monster" was reportedly seen. He also warned against disturbing the residents of the community.

"Anyone caught with a gun in that area better have a more solid excuse than hunting," Greer said.

Greer said many curiosity seekers have converged on the old Crank home about 10 miles south of Texarkana on Highway 71 where Bobby Ford, 25, former Ashdown resident, reported seeing the monster. Ford said the monster attacked him Saturday night after he and two other men said they shot at it several times with a shotgun.

Ford described the animal or monster as about seven feet tall, black and hairy, and said it runs on two feet.

Ford, his wife and several other members of the family, had lived in the house only five days when the incident occurred. He was treated early Sunday morning at St. Michael Hospital for shock and minor scratches.

Sheriff Greer said the Ford family had moved from the house and the house is vacant.

Constable Ernest Walraven of Fouke, who was called to the scene twice Saturday night, theorized that the monster may be a panther or a wolf. He said a

man living down the road from the home reported hearing something screaming like a woman back in the woods.

Walraven said he believes whatever kind of animal it was it was making its den under the house until the Fords moved in.

Sheriff Greer said his investigation has failed to turn up anything in connection with the monster report.

WANTED — Miller County Deputy Sheriff Roy Edwards of Fouke looks over a "composite drawing" of the "Fouke monster" which was posted on the bulletin board at the sheriff's office after the "monster" was reportedly seen last weekend. The Sheriff's Department will be on duty in the Fouke area this weekend checking "monster hunters" for guns and liquor, according to Sheriff Leslie Greer. (Staff Photo)

Fouke Monster news article from May 7, 1971
(Photo courtesy of the Texarkana Gazette)

1973 - Fouke

Mona Jackson was a young girl living in Fouke in 1973. She was only six or seven at the time but remembers the following incident very well because of its shocking nature. On the day in question, she rode her new bicycle up to the county road where they lived. She looked in both directions to make sure no cars were coming. When she did, she was startled to see a large, ape-like creature walking on two legs out of a pipeline clearing that intersected the road. She described it as being black in color with long arms and a broad chest. It was early evening, so she could see it clearly, although she did not absorb any details of its face, because she immediately turned and rode for the house as fast as she could. She had heard stories of the Fouke Monster for as long as she could remember, and to see something like that in person was a truly frightening experience. When Mona reached the house she was in such a panic, she could hardly open the door. She was sure the thing was an animal, not a person in a costume.

Source: Beau Jackson

The thick woods surrounding Fouke
(Photo by Lyle Blackburn)

April 2, 1974 - Fouke at Valley Gin

In 1974, William Richmond was living in Fouke, working as a hand on the Double-R Ranch. Richmond never envisioned himself living in Fouke, but he had just gotten out of the military and needed something to do. His father was a foreman on the ranch, so he was hired on to help out.

On the morning of April 2, Richmond and his brother decided to do some squirrel hunting. They got up early and hit the woods in an area known as "Valley Gin" south of Fouke. It wasn't long before they heard some squirrel chatter just inside a line of trees. Richmond told his brother to go ahead and find it while he finished smoking a cigarette. No sooner had his brother approached the trees, when "All hell broke loose," Richmond told me in an interview. "We started seeing the creature go through the woods. We could tell it was big and bipedal and running upright."

The brothers watched in amazement as the strange animal broke saplings and thrashed around as if it were angry. It also began to growl with a strange combination of whistling and low, guttural sounds. It was like nothing they'd ever heard or seen before.

Richmond told his brother they should leave immediately, but before they could turn and run, the creature rushed out in the open.

"When it charged us, I couldn't believe what I was seeing," Richmond recalled.

Now they had a full view of the creature as it stood approximately thirty yards away. Richmond described it as being at least seven feet tall and about four feet wide, with a heavy musculature, hairy body, and a rounded head. The men knew they didn't have enough firepower, but they fired anyway, fearing the thing was going to rush them. When the gun went off, the creature retreated back into the wood line, all the while howling with a blood-curdling scream. The brothers then backed up several yards, keeping their eye on it before finally turning and running for their truck, which was parked along a nearby road.

Richmond said they eventually regained their confidence. They decided to go home and get some high-powered rifles and a few friends and return to the area to see if they could find the creature again. When they got back, they found traces of large track indentions leading off into the woods. They followed them for a distance, but found no trace of the creature itself.

Source: Lyle Blackburn (interview with witness)

1974 - Doddridge

In 1974, Dave and Mike Giles and a friend were deer hunting south of Fouke when one of them bagged a big buck. They intended to clean the deer at home, so they placed it in the back of their truck and headed out. As they were driving up the small road that led to their house, a hairy, ape-like creature emerged from the woods and jumped onto the back of a motorcycle trailer they were towing. It proceeded to thrash about, damaging the two motorcycles strapped to the trailer's bed. When the driver realized what was happening, he hit the brakes and stopped the car. None of the men would get out of the cab. The creature looked enraged as it took its fury out on the bikes. After several seconds and considerable damage, it jumped off the trailer and ran back into the woods.

Source: Doyle Holmes

1974 - Fouke

Tony Nottingham left his home on County Road 8 to go deer hunting one afternoon in 1974. Woods engulfed the area at the time, so he could simply walk to his stand. As he was walking down the side of the road, a large, bipedal creature covered in black hair suddenly stepped out of the woods and started to cross the road. When it realized the hunter was there, it stopped and made eye contact. Nottingham said it was like a deer staring into headlights when they made eye contact, as if both were "dazzled" by what they were seeing.

Nottingham's surprise quickly turned to panic, however. He turned and ran straight back home. Even though the Fouke Monster was well known in town by then, Tony was still reluctant to tell anyone about his encounter for fear of ridicule. He kept the incident to himself for many years before telling anyone.

Source: Rickie Roberts

1977 - Days Creek

On a warm day in 1977, Will Lunsford spent the afternoon fishing in Days Creek near what was known as the "gravel pits." It was a sunny day, and Lunsford enjoyed the calm, peaceful atmosphere of the countryside deep in the recesses of wooded and swampy terrain that spread out west of Fouke. After several hours, Lunsford packed up his gear and began to walk back to his car, which was parked alongside one of the nearby county roads. As he walked, he began to hear what sounded like footsteps within the trees, but dismissed it as birds or some other type of small animal. The noise continued just out of sight, almost as if it were matching his own footfalls. Lunsford stopped a moment to listen. The sound in the woods stopped as well. When he resumed walking, the footsteps started again. Now the steps sounded too heavy to be a small animal. He thought perhaps it could be a panther, which was rather alarming since he was all alone.

Lunsford began walking faster, and as he did, the unseen thing increased its pace to match. It sounded like it was walking on two legs, though Lunsford doubted it could have been a person. Again he stopped walking, and again the thing stopped its own movement. Lunsford then broke out in a run, panicked at the thought of something unseen pacing him in the woods. As he ran, he could still hear noise in the woods, but it was hard to tell if the thing was still pacing him because of his own noisy footfalls. Lunsford crossed over a shallow portion of Days Creek and cut through some thick trees a short distance from his car. Suddenly a loud, high-pitched scream came from the woods. He did not know what kind of creature made the sound, but it was enough to hurry him into the vehicle without delay. He quickly started it up and left the area.

The incident left him shaken, but after a week his nerves finally calmed, and he was willing to return to the location for more fishing. If it were a panther, surely it would have moved on by then. Lunsford didn't take any chances, however, and packed a Bowie knife in his tackle box.

Lunsford arrived at Days Creek around 4:00 p.m. in the afternoon and proceeded to walk back to the same area as before. When he reached a section of the dirt road where it crossed over a pipeline clearing, he smelled a pungent, foul odor wafting through the air. It wasn't too unusual, however. Bobcats, coyotes, and other animals often pulled fish from the gravel pit ponds and left part of their remains rotting in the hot sun.

Lunsford went ahead through the woods and began to cross another pipeline toward his favorite pond, when he noticed what appeared to be a dark figure crouched at the tree line. As he focused, he could see it was something that had a limb pulled down in front of its face.

After a few moments, the animal stood up on two legs and looked right at the stunned fisherman. Its mouth was moving, apparently chewing leaves, which it must have been pulling from the limb. The thing was approximately seven to eight feet tall with a bulky frame, thick legs, long arms, and dark brown hair covering its body. Its eyes were dark and black as it stared at him for what was probably one to one and a half minutes total.

Lunsford stood frozen, literally "paralyzed with fear." The creature advanced a few steps, keeping his eyes on Lunsford the entire time. After about thirty seconds, it returned to the same tree, crouched back down, and resumed eating. A short time later, it stood up again and simply turned and walked into the woods. At that point, Lunsford gathered his wits and took off running down the pipeline clearing as far away from the thing as he could get. He feared the creature might trail him in the woods as he presumed it had done before, but Lunsford never heard anything or saw the creature again. When he finally reached his truck, he jumped inside and locked the door. Seconds later he burst into tears. The whole event had been unbelievable and shocking.

Lunsford initially told a few trusted friends and family members, but at the time they mostly reacted with snickers and teasing. As a result, Lunsford resolved to keep his story quiet until years later when people began to take the subject of Sasquatch more seriously. Now he spends hours in the woods around Fouke hoping to prove what he had seen all those years ago.

FOUKE FACTS: The location where Lunsford claims to have seen the Fouke creature is very close to the lake where Lynn Crabtree had his seminal sighting back in the 1960s. See entry *1965 – Jonesville (Crabtree Lake)*.

Source: Lyle Blackburn (personal interview)

1978 - Fouke

Sometime between 1978 and the early 1980s, Fouke resident Crockie Pilgreen had saved enough money to buy himself a small home south of Fouke, where he could start a better life of his own. He had previously lived within the town limits, but was eager to get out to the countryside. The home he purchased was not fancy by any means, but it was comfortable with a modest plot of land. There was even a pond located behind the house.

Shortly after purchasing the property, however, Mr. Pilgreen saw something he never expected. One evening while he was doing dishes at the kitchen sink, he looked out the window and noticed something crouched down on the far side of the pond. At first he wasn't sure what it was, but finally it raised its torso and head as it took a drink of water from its hand. It was some kind of ape-like animal that he could only assume was the Fouke Monster. Pilgreen watched in fright as the thing took another drink and then walked off into the woods.

The next day he returned to town, where he rented a small apartment. He never returned to the home.

Source: John Attaway

3.

Modern
Encounters

After the heyday of *The Legend of Boggy Creek* played out in the 1970s, the media gradually lost interest. As a result, publicized news reports of the Fouke Monster dropped off considerably in the 1980s. This led many to believe that sightings of the creature had stopped. This is not the case, however. Sightings in and around Fouke did continue, but the details were only circulated by word of mouth. Later, as sightings surged in the 1990s and beyond, new outlets for publicizing them were beginning to appear in the form of Smokey Crabtree's later books and Bigfoot-related websites on the World Wide Web. Through my own research, I have been able to document numerous reports, both new and old, which establish not only have the sightings continued all along, but the mystery of the Fouke Monster is far from over.

1980s

1980s - Fouke at Boggy Creek

In the early 1980s, Ronda Cornett and several other Fouke residents saw something fitting the description of the Fouke Monster near a large dirt pile at their home near the origin of Boggy Creek.

FOUKE FACTS: Boggy Creek's origin is located near County Road 9 south of Fouke's main intersection.

Source: Lyle Blackburn (personal interview)

1980s - Mercer Bayou

Harry Elrod said he was checking his trotline in the Mercer Bayou area known as "The Deadening," at around 10:00 p.m. when he saw something he can never get out of this mind. It was a clear night with a sliver of moonlight illuminating the black water. Elrod was in his boat with the motor off, kneeling in the front of the craft so he could pull up the line to check each drop for fish. As he pulled on the line, he suddenly felt a "strong tug" on the far end. Elrod hurried along with excitement, thinking it must be a really big fish. When he got to the point of resistance, however, he couldn't lift the line out of the water there. Figuring it was probably a snag, he started to cut the line when "a tall, hairy figure rose from the water with the line in its hand."

Elrod dropped the line and reeled back in horror. He then jumped into the shallow water and scrambled to the bank as fast as he could. From there he ran several miles through the woods until he came to a house on Blackmon Ferry Road. He knocked on the door and pleaded with the owners to let him use the phone to call the Miller County Sheriff's Office. A deputy responded and subsequently investigated the area where he'd been working the trotline, but could find no trace of the creature. Elrod thought it was strange that he had caught no fish over the last few days. Perhaps the creature, in its hunger, had been stealing them from the line.

Source: Texas Bigfoot Research Center

February 20, 1982 - Jonesville

It was an unseasonably warm afternoon on February 20, 1982. Fifteen-year-old Terry Sutton had collected a jarful of night crawlers from his mother's garden and headed off with his fishing gear toward the pond on the far side of his family's property. Their home was located in Jonesville, just off the main road that connects their countryside community with the outside world. Having grown up in the Jonesville/Fouke area, Terry was no stranger to the lurid tales of their haunting, hair-covered beast, but this was not something that crossed his mind very often when traversing the backwoods. Like most boys in the area, Terry was an experienced hunter, trapper, and fisherman who had spent countless hours in the rich bayous. He was very familiar with all varieties of local wildlife and would not likely mistake one for a seven-foot-tall, hairy hominoid. Perhaps that is why this event would be so shocking to him.

After traversing the quarter mile from his home to the pond, Terry loaded his gear into the small aluminum boat his dad kept there and pushed off into the lazy water. He baited a hook with one of the fat worms, dropped it into the water, and sat there quietly fishing for the rest of the afternoon.

As he sat there fishing and enjoying the solitude, he heard something moving through the thick blanket of leaves that covered the late winter ground. Earlier, he had heard what he thought was the bellowing of his uncle's old Black Angus bull who roamed the adjacent property, so naturally he assumed the bull had wandered toward the pond. That, or perhaps his father was coming down to check on him. Either way, the sound was nothing out of the ordinary, since anything walking through the leaves would have made a significant amount of noise.

About an hour before dusk, Terry decided to paddle the boat around a small bend in the pond where the fishing might be better. The bend was like a small neck of water that jutted off into a wooded area. He heard some more loud rustling in the leaves coming from that direction, but still he wasn't alarmed...until he rounded the bend. Now he could see the source of the leafy noise. It was a large, hair-covered animal walking on two legs across a small embankment near the pond. Its back was facing Terry as it headed toward a ravine that dipped down to a nearby creek.

"It was walking away in a casual stroll," Terry told me in a personal interview. "At first, I couldn't believe what I was seeing."

Terry was a mere sixty feet from the creature, so there was no mistake that he was seeing something other than human, bear, or any other common animal. Terry was over six feet tall at the time, so he estimated the creature's height to be as tall or taller than he was. He described its fur as being scraggly, three to five inches long, and colored a dull black or very dark brown. It had notably long arms that swung as it walked, giving it an ape-like quality, although it did not hunch over as an ape might do.

"I know there's varying stories, but what I saw was not bent over. It was walking upright just as straight as I do," Terry recalled. In addition to the physical attributes, Terry also remembered smelling a musky odor.

Terry sat in the boat for several seconds—though it seemed more like an eternity—as he watched the creature walk by. During this time it never looked back, presumably because it never heard the boy floating quietly on the pond. A few moments later, the creature walked over the bank and disappeared into a ravine leading to the creek bottom below. The thing was now completely out of sight, but Terry could still hear its footsteps in the leaves as it continued to walk. Terry quickly paddled to the bank and got out of the boat. At that point, the creature's footsteps stopped. Terry stood frozen, listening intently in the direction of the ravine. Then he heard the creature start running!

"I didn't panic until I heard it start running," Terry confessed. "It was pretty much nervousness until then, but once I heard it run, fear overwhelmed me, and I took off running for the house."

Terry arrived at the house out of breath and still holding the boat paddle in his hand. He told his mother what he had seen, and she immediately called his father. Lloyd Sutton pulled into the driveway a short time later.

"Just as I parked, before I got out, Terry came out of the house and was standing near the edge of the patio with his hands over his face," Mr. Sutton told me in a personal interview. "I could tell immediately that there was something wrong. I had no idea what it was, but I could see that something was not right. I stepped out of my pickup and said, 'Terry what's the matter?' He said, 'Dad, I just saw the Fouke Monster!'"

After Terry calmed down and explained what he had seen, Mr. Sutton felt he should head down to the pond to investigate. He quickly gathered his .357 Magnum pistol, a 35 mm camera, and two flashlights. "I asked Terry if he wanted to go with me, but I could tell he was a little hesitant. I told him it might be better to go on back down there and get it over with, or he would always want to shy away from there," Mr. Sutton explained. Terry was reluctant, but with his father's encouragement, he agreed.

The Suttons walked the quarter mile down to the pond as dusk hovered heavy over Jonesville. They immediately looked for any signs of tracks, but found nothing in the dry blanket of leaves or on the water's edge. They followed the creature's path down into the ravine and checked along the creek bank. They found no tracks but did detect the faint remnants of a foul animal odor. As Mr. Sutton put it: "I can't describe it, nor have I ever smelled anything like it, as I can remember. It may have been a little agitated after hearing Terry bump the bank with his boat earlier, and the running may have contributed to the odor, I don't know. But it was for real. You could walk either direction from that spot, and it would go away. It was just lingering there in the moist air of the creek bottom."

By now, darkness had enveloped the woods, making it difficult to continue the investigation, but they walked back to the pond and looked around once more. While walking west along the bank, a large animal suddenly tore out the brush and ran in front of them just out of sight. They pointed their flashlights in the direction of the animal but did not get a glimpse of it.

"I jumped across the water and took off after it with Terry right behind me," Mr. Sutton said. "We were making so much noise running, I would say: 'Stop!' We could hear it straight ahead of us and would go again. Each time we would stop, we could still hear it, but then the last time we stopped… nothing. We walked around in circles from the last time we heard it, but we didn't hear or see anything again."

With that, the Suttons trekked through the darkness back to the house and spent the rest of the evening talking about the incident. Terry kept the incident a secret for a long time but eventually mentioned it to some friends. He was ribbed, laughed at, and called a liar on many occasions, but he never changed his story. During my initial research into the Fouke Monster case, several people told me about Terry's sighting, saying his family was well respected and I should try to follow up on it. Mr. Sutton was a longtime deacon in the local church, and although some people laughed off the incident, most felt Terry and his father were not the type to make up stories, especially knowing how easily it could become a source of ridicule.

FOUKE FACTS: The pond is still there on the Sutton property, and I have visited it many times over the years as I have gotten to know the family better. I consider Terry's sighting to be one of the best I have ever investigated.

Source: Lyle Blackburn (personal interviews)

The pond where Terry Sutton was fishing when he saw the creature
(Photo by Lloyd Sutton)

June 1982 - Sulphur River

In June of 1982, Jerry Scoggins dropped by to check on his boat, which was tied up near the Sulphur River south of Jonesville. After resecuring it, he began to head back through the trees on his way home but stopped when he heard something splashing in the water. Figuring it must be a large alligator, he turned around to get a look, only to see a large, hairy man-like animal moving across the river. It splashed through the water, walked up on the bank, and disappeared into the trees.

Source: Terry Sutton

November 18, 1984 - Fouke

In the fall of 1984, a local hunter was walking into the Sulphur River Wildlife Management Area on his way to hunt when a horse and four cows came running up a hill toward him. They appeared to be in a state of distress or panic as they fled into a pine thicket. The man followed in the direction they were fleeing, and when he reached a swampy area, he could see a "large creature at least seven feet tall with long, dark brown hair all over its body." It was standing on two legs, thigh-deep in the swamp some distance away.

When the animal saw the hunter, it immediately walked out of sight. The hunter attempted to pursue it. He had heard the legend of the Fouke Monster throughout his life but until now did not truly believe it. The hunter saw the creature again, and this time, he raised his rifle and aimed through the scope. However, the animal moved again before he was able to sight it into the crosshairs. After it disappeared the second time, the hunter became afraid, thinking perhaps there were more creatures nearby. In a report filed with the Gulf Coast Bigfoot Research Organization, the man said:

> *Moments after it disappeared terror set in, and I began wondering if there were others nearby. I quickly got back to my vehicle and left. I still haven't gone back and probably never will. Why I was going to shoot it, I don't know? But today I am glad that I did not.*

Source: Gulf Coast Bigfoot Research Organization

1985 - Jonesville

Over the years, a number of families living in and around Fouke raised chickens as part of their farm or livestock business. One morning around 1985, a young man living in the small community of Jonesville went out to check on the large chicken coop located on his family's property. As he approached the building, he could see a large, ape-like animal trying to get inside. Once the creature caught sight of the witness, it quickly ran into the woods.

Source: John Attaway

September 1986 - Fouke at Boggy Creek

In the fall of 1986, Fouke resident Eddie Burgess was driving a representative from a major beer brewing company to a wheat field located on the back side of his property. The Burgess family owns a large tract of land in Fouke that contains a considerable segment of Boggy Creek. Upon reaching the back gate, Burgess stopped the truck and got out to unlock it. At that point he noticed a tall, hair-covered figure walking toward them approximately eighty yards away. When the creature saw the men, it immediately turned and headed down an incline toward Boggy Creek. The brewing company representative jumped out of the truck and both men watched as the creature crossed the creek and disappeared into the shadowy woods beyond. The guest was shocked and confused by the sighting. Eddie Burgess was not. He and his family had lived on the property for many years and were very familiar with what they already knew was lurking along the infamous creek that runs through their property.

FOUKE FACTS: Members of the Burgess family claim to have had several experiences with the creature over the years. At one point, the family was so fearful of the creature lurking around their property, they installed a removable board across the front door for extra security. They jokingly referred to it as "the monster blocker." But according to the family, their encounters were no laughing matter. (Also see entry *January 15, 2000*.)

Source: Lyle Blackburn (personal interview)

*The portion of Boggy Creek that runs through the Burgess property
(Photo by Lyle Blackburn)*

May 1987 - Fouke at Boggy Creek

On a moonless night in May 1987, James "Peanut" Jones
and his wife were frog gigging in a pond located close to Boggy
Creek. As they quietly rowed their boat along the edges of the
pond searching for frogs, they heard something large moving in
the brush beyond. Jones shined a spotlight in the direction of
the noise and was surprised to see a pair of brightly illuminated
eyes staring back at him. Curious to know what kind of animal
was watching them, they rowed toward it to get a better view.
After a few paddles, Jones could make out the shadowy shape of a
large creature. As they got closer, the animal began to move in the
trees. It appeared to be man-like and walking upright. Inevitably,
thoughts of the Fouke Monster popped into his mind, and that
was enough to make him drop the light and begin rowing to the

opposite edge of the pond. Once they reached the bank, Jones and his wife jumped out and pulled the boat ashore. They grabbed a few things and ran to their four-wheeler, fired up the ignition, and headed up the trail out of the bottoms.

FOUKE FACTS: The location of this incident was very close to the spot where Eddie Burgess had a sighting eight months earlier. Boggy Creek runs through the same property where the pond is located. (See previous entry.)

Source: Lyle Blackburn (personal interview)

1990s

October 22, 1990 - Fouke at Sulphur River

According to a report published in the *Texarkana Gazette*, two men from Oklahoma, Jim Walls and Charles Humbert, were traveling north on Highway 71 on October 22, 1990. As they approached the Sulphur River Bridge around 8:30 a.m., they got wind of a pungent odor that was strong enough to make them pull over. They thought there might be a large dead animal in the vicinity. After stopping on the gravel shoulder just before the bridge, something off to the right caught their eye. It was a tall, man-like creature covered in shaggy, black hair running across an open field toward the south riverbank, east of the highway.

"He [ran] upright just like a human, not like a bear or gorilla," Jim Walls told reporters. "I don't know what I saw, but I know it had to be made of flesh, blood, and bone."

The men estimated its height to be eight feet and its weight approximately four hundred pounds. They described its face as looking "much more human-like than a chimpanzee or a monkey."

After the creature ran approximately two hundred yards across the field, it paused for a moment and then leapt from the high riverbank toward the water. The men quickly drove across the bridge and circled back to see if they could get another look, but the creature was already gone. Walls assumed it must have jumped into the river and disappeared below the surface, but this was pure speculation since they never actually saw it hit the water.

Walls and Humbert attempted to get permission from some of the local landowners so they could continue their search, but they were turned down in all cases.

"We went driving down some dirt trails, but no one would let us on their property," Walls said. "They seemed more concerned about keeping outsiders away than about any monster."

The men were convinced they had witnessed something truly strange. "I don't know what it was, to tell you the truth," Humbert concluded. "But it chilled my bones."

FOUKE FACTS: The article goes on to quote Sheriff H.L. Phillips, who said his office had received at least one sighting per month during 1990.

Source: *Texarkana Gazette*

October 1992 - Fouke at McKinney Bayou

On a cold, foggy night in October 1992, five young men were driving on a lonely stretch of road south of Fouke at around 11:00 p.m. They had just passed an area known as McKinney Bayou when they noticed the bright headlights of a semi-truck coming toward them. As the truck got closer, they caught a glimpse of someone—or something—as it came out of the shadows and walked across the road in full view of both vehicles. The figure formed a dark silhouette in the headlights, but they could clearly see it was some kind of large, hairy animal walking upright on two legs. The creature had come from the thick woods that lined one side of the road and was headed toward an open field that lay on the opposite side. The driver slowed their car to a stop. The truck did the same.

The witnesses' first impression was it must surely be a bear, but as they continued to watch the creature stroll across the road a mere fifty yards away, they realized it was not. It was more man-like, but larger than a man, standing an estimated seven feet tall and walking on two legs the entire time. It never paused or looked at the cars; it just kept moving. Facial features and other fine de-tails were hard to see because of the silhouette effect, but the men were certain the creature was not an ordinary animal.

"It was definitely taller and thicker than a man and bushy like it had a thick coat of hair," Rusty Anderson recalled. He was one of the five men in the car that night.

After taking a few long strides, the figure left the road and en-tered a field where it moved beyond the reach of the headlights. At that point, the truck driver hurriedly got out of his vehicle, as did the five young men. They tried to get another look at the uniden-tified creature, but it had already disappeared into the darkness.

The men spoke with the trucker, all of whom were astounded by what they had just seen. The driver of the car was simply in awe. He and the other four passengers, including Rusty Anderson, lived in the general area, so they had certainly heard stories of the Fouke Monster many times and felt perhaps they had just seen the animal for themselves. The truck driver, however, had never heard the legend. He was shocked by the backstory.

The incident was so surreal, the men discussed the possibility of having been hoaxed. But in the end, they did not feel this was the case. They were certain it was a real animal and not a person in a costume. After a last look into the field, the parties returned to their vehicles and went their separate ways.

Source: Lyle Blackburn (personal interviews with two of the witnesses)

1992 - Fouke

Around 1992, Ben Morgan observed a hairy, upright creature standing beside the road as he drove at night.

Source: Lyle Blackburn (personal interview)

1993 - Fouke

According to Dorothy Briggs, who worked at a convenience store in Fouke during the early 1990s, two gentlemen came in one night well after midnight, sometime around 1993. They had been traveling on Highway 71 en route to Shreveport when they spotted something very strange crossing the road near Fouke. The two men, one of whom was Roosevelt Shine from Memphis, claimed to have no prior knowledge of the Fouke Monster.

As the two men drove south along Highway 71, they saw what Mr. Shine described as "some kind of ape-man" walk out of the woods and onto the road in front of them. Shine slowed the vehicle until they rolled to stop about one hundred feet from the creature, which had paused on the shoulder of the road, eyeing the approaching headlights. As they sat there in growing disbelief, the men could see the creature was definitely walking on two legs, covered with dark hair, and standing approximately seven feet tall. It seemed adept in its movements, so it was fairly clear it was some sort of bipedal animal and not merely a bear who had taken to walking upright.

Moments later, another car approached from the opposite direction and came to a stop. The occupants had also noticed the strange creature, now frozen like a deer in the headlights. The couple in the car were from Fouke and were well aware of its namesake monster, but they never believed they would see such a thing. The creature continued to stand at the side of the road, wary of the growing audience, when incredibly, a semi-truck came up alongside the Fouke couple and stopped to see what was happening. The witnesses now totaled five adults.

A few moments later, the creature darted back into the woods, running fast on two legs. All five people got out of their parked vehicles and began to discuss what had just taken place. To everyone's amazement, they all saw what was very clearly a creature fitting the description of the Fouke Monster. After some conversation, they decided to report the incident to the local authorities, which they did. Afterward, Mr. Shine and his companion made their way to the convenience store in Fouke where they told their story to the clerk, who eventually put them in touch with Smokey Crabtree.

Source: Smokey Crabtree

1993 - Fouke

Four hours after the previous sighting and only a half mile away (see previous entry), a woman saw an animal fitting the description of the Fouke Monster cross County Road 10 in the early morning hours.

Source: Smokey Crabtree

Summer 1996 - Fouke at Boggy Creek

A young Alex Burgess was playing outside in "the yard" with his sister when he heard something moving through the brush just inside a line of trees that surrounded their home. (The yard was essentially a clearing behind the family home that backed up to a wooded area near Boggy Creek. Their father, Eddie Burgess, kept the area clear using a brush hog, but much of the terrain on their property is/was heavy woods interspersed with open fields.) When Alex heard the noise, he looked up and saw a large, hairy creature walking by, about five yards into the trees. The creature was walking perpendicular to the children using its arms to clear a path through the brush and vines as it walked on two legs. There were trails going through the woods, but for whatever reason, the creature chose to walk right through the brush. The creature never looked at Burgess; it merely walked by and eventually disappeared from sight as it got further away. Alex was quite young at the time, but feels confident he saw what he believes might have been the Fouke Monster.

FOUKE FACTS: The witness's father, Eddie Burgess, also claims to have had sightings on the property and believes one or more of these creatures is responsible for other incidents over the last twenty-five years. (See entries *September 1986* and *January 15, 2000*.)

Source: Lyle Blackburn (personal interview)

November 1996 - Fouke at Sulphur River

In the late-night hours of November 1996, a truck driver was traveling north on Highway 71, having made an earlier delivery in Shreveport. The sky was overcast, but the halogen headlights of his eighteen-wheeler effectively carved away the darkness as he rolled across the lonely blacktop. The trip had been uneventful until approximately 1:00 a.m., when he neared the Sulphur River Bridge that crosses the highway eight miles south of Fouke. As he drew closer, his eyes were drawn to a tall, dark shape standing near the water on the right-hand side of the road. At first he believed it to be a dead tree trunk, but then he noticed the shape had two red eyes reflecting back in the headlights. Suddenly the "tree" began walking away from the river bank toward the woods. The driver was both startled and curious, so he let off his throttle to slow down. The creature looked to be dull gray in color, like that of a dead tree. As it walked away on two legs, it took huge steps, covering the ground quickly without any noticeable arm movement. As the truck continued to slow, the brakes made a deep rumbling sound. At that point, the driver heard a loud scream coming from the direction of the creature, before it disappeared from view in the darkness. The startled driver accelerated and left the area without stopping in Fouke.

It was only later that the truck driver was able to do some Internet research, finding others had reported an unexplained creature in the area. Prior to that, he had only associated Sasquatch sightings with the Pacific Northwest.

Source: Connor Ameigh

September 17, 1997 - Fouke at Boggy Creek

On September 17, 1997, a man living north of Boggy Creek on the west side of Fouke was outside tending to his lawn and working on his car. At around 6:00 p.m., he began to feel uneasy. It was as if he were being watched, but initially he could not figure out the source of the strange feeling. It wasn't until he looked into the surrounding woods that he noticed something moving in the brush. When he walked toward the woods, he saw a large, dark brown creature. He described it as being "about seven feet tall with a dark black face."

The man watched the creature for several minutes before deciding to retrieve his pistol from the house. By the time he got back, the creature was no longer visible, so he walked slowly toward the woods in an attempt to get another look. Finally, he spotted it sitting on the ground about thirty feet from where he had first seen it. By his estimation, he was roughly two hundred feet from it. The witness stood there for some time watching the animal, until the sun finally dropped behind the horizon and the animal was engulfed by the encroaching darkness. The man's wife returned from a shopping trip shortly thereafter, so he quickly ushered her into the house. They did not see any further sign of the creature.

Source: Gulf Coast Bigfoot Research Organization

July 11, 1998 - Jonesville

On July 11, 1998 around 9:00 a.m., a woman was babysitting her sister's children in the Jonesville area southwest of Fouke. Eager to enjoy the day before the unbearable summer heat set in, she decided to take the children on a walk to an area where some new timber had been cut. When they arrived at the spot, the woman noticed a strange figure in the trees to her right. As she focused on it, she realized it was a "very large hairy creature" watching them from the edge of the woods. The woman became frightened, but managed to keep her composure as she immediately hurried the kids back toward the house. In the process, she kept looking over her shoulder to see if the thing was following them. Luckily, it was not.

Source: Gulf Coast Bigfoot Research Organization

2000s

January 15, 2000 - Fouke at Boggy Creek

On January 15, 2000, Fouke resident Eddie Burgess saw a "hairy, man-like creature" walking through a wheat field near Boggy Creek at approximately three o'clock in the afternoon. The Burgess family owns a large tract of land in Fouke that contains a considerable segment of Boggy Creek. The creature appeared to have thick, reddish-brown hair that was matted with sticks and leaves. Burgess also caught a "distinct musky smell" wafting downwind from the animal. The creature stopped and looked at the witness before disappearing into the thick trees surrounding Boggy Creek.

"I was very frightened when it stopped and looked in my direction," Burgess said. "I had a gun, but would never shoot anything unless it is game."

FOUKE FACTS: Members of the Burgess family claim to have had several experiences with the creature over the years. At one point, the family was so fearful of the creature lurking around their property, they installed a removable board across the front door for extra security. They jokingly referred to it as "the monster blocker." But according to the family, their encounters were no laughing matter. (Also see entry *September 1986*.)

Sources: Lyle Blackburn (personal interview)

October 2000 - Sulphur River

In October 2000, Stacy Hudson was scouting areas south of Fouke where he could hunt for deer. Hudson was an avid bow-hunter who had spent many hours hunting in the woods of Texas and Arkansas. He finally located a good spot along the Sulphur River, where he hung his tree stand in a small oak about twelve feet off the ground. He then left the area for the evening, as he intended to return the next morning to hunt.

The next morning before sunrise, Hudson made his way back to the area and parked his vehicle. The air was cool and crisp, so he changed into his warmest camo coveralls and sprayed down with a scent-killer product to remove any foreign smells. He then grabbed his bow and used a green-hued flashlight to make his way to the tree stand in the dark. When he arrived, he found the top portion of the stand was twisted around to the back of the tree and the bottom was moved to the base of the tree. It was odd, but finding no explanation for it, Hudson fixed the tree stand, climbed up, and settled in to wait.

By now it was about 5:30 a.m. It was still not light, but the moon was full enough that Hudson could somewhat see in the dark. He sat silent and still with his bow in his lap. The arrows were pointing away from him, resting on the tree stand's gun rest. Everything was camouflaged except the silvery broadhead tips on the ends of his arrows.

As Hudson sat in the blackness, he heard something walk up behind him. He turned slowly to see if he could get a look. He could only tell it was something big and black. It was much too large to be a hog, so he thought perhaps it was a stray cow. He sat still, hoping it would leave so it wouldn't scare away the deer. Then something brushed across Hudson's leg. He hadn't heard anything climb up the tree under him, so he simply remained still and looked forward.

Suddenly, a huge hand reached up and grabbed for the exposed broadheads. The hand was "shiny black, and the fingers were huge!" Hudson recalled. The palms were also black like those of a gorilla. When the hand closed around the razor-sharp broadheads, the thing screamed in pain. The sound was loud, like a bull, but definitely not a bull.

Hudson was so frightened, he yelled loudly in an attempt to scare off whatever it was. He was essentially helpless—in the dark, in a tree stand. The injured thing immediately took off running, breaking trees and tearing up everything in its path as it went. It was apparently just as frightened and alarmed as the hunter.

Hudson tried to calm his nerves as he waited for daylight. Once the sun rose enough to see, Hudson quickly left the area and did not return.

FOUKE FACTS: Hudson's incident was reenacted on the "Swamp Stalker" episode of the television show, *MonsterQuest*. On another occasion, Hudson heard a strange tree-knocking sound, which he believes might have been made by the creature.

Sources: Lyle Blackburn (personal interview)

The Sulphur River, known as the "Arkansas Amazon"
(Photo by Lyle Blackburn)

Winter 2000 - Mercer Bayou

One of the most dramatic encounters with the alleged beast was reported by a coon hunter. On a cold, moonlit night in the winter of 2000, he and several other men were hunting in an area of Mercer known as Thornton Wells. At some point, one of the hunter's dogs treed a raccoon deep in the swamp. He followed his dog's lead and separated from the other men. After locating the raccoon and collecting his dog, the hunter started back across the swamp to rejoin the group when he heard something "walking in the flooded timber." Thinking it was one of his fellow hunters, the man called out.

"To my dismay no one answered—instead all I heard was a deep throated gurgling growl and [smelled] the awfullest [*sic*] putrid smell," he explained. "I also heard a whining kind of a whistling sound."

The dogs began whimpering and cowering behind the hunter's legs, which struck him as very unusual for such experienced hounds. The hunter was puzzled but unconcerned, so he gathered his dogs and started back across the swamp.

"After a few minutes I heard this sound of someone or something walking in the water again," he continued. "So I stopped and turned around and standing right behind me was a creature of immense size." The thing was hulking and huge, covered in dark, rusty-brown hair that was wet and matted. The skin on its face and hands was "gray and leathery," and while its overall characteristics were ape-like, its face was "like that of a person." It stood upright on two legs in the shallow water as it flashed its teeth at the awestruck man. His recollection is chilling:

> *I don't ever remember being that scared. He made a hissing sound and reached down and took his hand and started scooping water and throwing it up at me and making a deep throaty noise. My dogs started chomping at the leash and growling trying to get at it, having regained*

their bravery. I grabbed the leash and tore out across that swamp so scared that, for a while, I went in the wrong direction. I got to a big cypress knee and caught my breath. I could hear the thing behind me, it sounded like it was about a 100 yards or so back. It followed me for a ways, then after a while I could hear it across the bayou making a moaning sound and moving away slowly.

I got my breath and my compass and my bearings and started back to the truck. When I got there I didn't say a word to my friends about what I saw and heard for fear they would laugh me down. Needless to say I never returned to Thornton Wells nor do I plan to. For a long time I kept this to myself. I even had nightmares about it.

Source: Texas Bigfoot Research Center

2000 or 2001 - Fouke

Another incident supposedly occurred sometime between 2000 and 2001. Denny Roberts was at the Monster Mart convenience store in Fouke (which he currently owns) when he spoke to a man who was doing survey work for the Army Corps of Engineers as they prepared the site for the new Highway 549 construction project. According to the man, he had been working in a wooded area somewhere south of Fouke when he came upon the remains of a large, hairy animal. The carcass was already starting to decay, giving off a foul odor, but still he could tell it had been roughly the size of a large man and covered with a layer of dark, matted fur. It did not appear to be a bear or any familiar animal, but there was nothing he could really do at the time to determine what it might be. The man claimed when he returned to the site the following day to continue his work, the carcass was gone. Apparently the man was not familiar with the stories of the Fouke

Monster, as the subject only came up while discussing strange things he had seen while working in the area.

Source: Denny and Rickie Roberts

2001 - Mercer Lake

While Rickie Roberts, former owner of the Monster Mart convenience store, was working at the store, a hunter told him he came face-to-face with a large, ape-like creature while hunting near Mercer Lake south of Fouke. He was so frightened by the encounter he dropped his expensive rifle and ran from the woods. He refused to return to the area, even to retrieve his gun. The incident occurred near the old train trestle that spans across the Sulphur River just west of Highway 71. (Remnants of the old structure still remain today, although the railway has long since been removed.)

A short time later, while showing some out-of-town visitors around, Rickie brought them to a location on Highway 71 where the train trestles are visible from the road. He pulled over and pointed out it had been the site of several eyewitness reports. As they were looking, they noticed a dark figure standing in the trees just east of the trestle columns. Its movements did not seem consistent with that of a bear, so they tried to get a better look. By the time they got closer to investigate, the figure was gone.

Source: Rickie Roberts

2001 - Mercer Bayou at Thornton Wells

Sometime in 2001, Billy Attaway said he was drift fishing in Mercer Bayou near the Thornton Wells boat ramp when he smelled a horrible odor. He looked up and scanned the bank to see if he could find the source. When he did, he saw a large, hair-covered thing watching him from the trees. It appeared to be standing on two legs. Attaway was so frightened, he paddled to the middle of the bayou channel, where he waited until it was gone. After a good while, he finally paddled back to the ramp, got his boat out, and quickly left the area.

Source: Rickie Roberts

Mercer Bayou at Thornton Wells
(Photo by Lyle Blackburn)

2003 - Jonesville

According to Miller County Sheriff, H.L. Phillips, he took a report in 2003 from a family in Jonesville who said their two children had been out riding bikes when they came upon what they described as a "hairy monster" during the evening hours. The kids were quite shaken and quickly pedaled away on their bikes. When they returned home and frantically told their mother, she decided to contact the authorities. The sheriff's office took the report seriously, as they always did back then, and asked if she thought the children had seen the Fouke Monster. The woman was puzzled. They were new to the area, having only lived there a short time. Neither she nor the kids had ever heard of the Fouke Monster.

Source: Retired Sheriff H.L. Phillips

April 2004 - Carter Lake (Mercer Bayou)

In April 2004, Doyle Holmes was fishing in the area known as Carter Lake at the southern tip of Mercer Bayou. About one hour after sunrise, he heard some movement and splashing on the nearby bank. Figuring it might be a large hog, he peered into the trees trying to get a glimpse of it. After a few moments he caught sight of something, but it definitely was not a four-legged hog. Whatever it was walked on two legs. Holmes could not get a clear view of its upper body due to the overhanging canopies of cypress, but he was able to see the figure from about the thigh down to the calf. There was no doubt it was a bipedal creature, but in the shadows, Holmes could not completely rule out a man in a pair of fishing waders. However, Holmes had been out on the lake since before daylight and hadn't seen any sign of other people, not even a boat parked on the edge of the water. This was notable since the area was not accessible by any means other than by boat. He was a good distance from the nearest road and could not imagine how a human could have been walking on the bank so far out, since it was miles from the nearest home.

FOUKE FACTS: This location is not far from a spot known as "The Mound" where an old hermit named Herb Jones once lived. Jones and his residence (essentially a small shack) were featured in *The Legend of Boggy Creek* movie. Doyle and his son Nathan would discover several large, five-toed footprints in this same area seven months later. See the *Carter Lake* entry in **The Evidence** chapter for details.

Source: Lyle Blackburn (personal interview)

May 2009 - Long Slough / Smith Park

In the spring of 2009, Texarkana wildlife photographer, Jennifer Bland, was driving the back roads of the Sulphur River area looking for subjects to photograph. She was driving slowly down a dirt road leading from Smith Park to Long Slough at around 2:00 p.m. when a large, bipedal animal ran out of the woods, took a few bounding steps, and disappeared into the trees on the other side. She could see it was brown in color and ran on two legs the entire time. It also appeared to have an elongated snout.

The incident was so strange and unexpected, Bland just sat in the car for several minutes pondering what she had seen. Suddenly, an "unearthly scream" came from the woods where the thing had run. It was so unnerving, she turned her car around and quickly left the area.

Although the sighting was brief, she had a good view of the subject in broad daylight. She was confident it was not a typical animal or a person. As a wildlife photographer, she had seen every type of wild animal Arkansas had to offer. This was not one she had seen before.

FOUKE FACTS: The description of an "elongated snout" is rather puzzling, since it is not a characteristic normally associated with the Fouke Monster. However, it is typical of a cryptid class called "Dogmen." I have never heard of a Dogman report in the area, so unless it's something other than a typical Southern Bigfoot, I can only conjecture the creature might have had something in its mouth—perhaps a squirrel or rabbit—making it appear to have a longer snout.

Source: Lyle Blackburn (personal interview)

*The road to Long Slough where Jennifer Bland
saw the unidentified creature
(Photo by Lyle Blackburn)*

2010 to Present

May 2010 - Fouke

In May 2010, just before 11:00 p.m., Michael and Liz Row-ton were driving home on a county road north of Fouke's main strip. Liz had been working the late shift at a local establishment, and her husband had picked her up. It had been raining that day, but by the late evening it had dissipated into a fine mist that covered Fouke in a dreary haze. The mist glistened as the headlights blazed across the wet macadam, but visibility was not a problem. After traveling a mile or so down the long, winding pavement that cuts its way through a mass of thick trees on either side, they passed a small cluster of oil wells in a clearing on the left side of the road. As they approached, Michael noticed something ahead squatting in the grassy area between the edge of the road and the wall of trees. Caught in the headlights, the thing stood up and quickly ran across the road a mere twenty yards in front of them. It was so sudden that Liz was looking down at the time and did not see the creature. However, she knew something had happened when Michael abruptly slowed down and craned his head in the direction of the strange runner.

Alarmed, Liz asked her husband what was going on. In a tone of utter disbelief, he simply said: "I think I saw the Fouke Monster." The look on his face told her he was not playing a joke. She urged him to turn around so they could get another look. Michael immediately did a 180 in the road. The headlights spilled into the trees where he had seen the creature run. Scanning the lighted area for any sign of the creature, they caught a glimpse of its shadowy outline as it stood just inside the cover of tall pines. Michael eased the car forward, but the animal—or whatever it was—quickly disappeared from sight.

By now, Liz thought better of any further investigation, feeling a surge of fear replace the initial whirlwind of excitement. The brief glimpse of the shadowy figure had given her the creeps. Knowing it could still be watching them, she insisted they get out of there and only come back when it was daylight to investigate. Michael agreed as he spun the car around and hit the gas. He had no idea what he had just seen, but it was definitely something he could not explain.

The couple described the creature as being approximately seven feet tall, covered in dark hair, and running upright on two legs. Michael had the best view, but in the scant few seconds he saw it running, he was not able to make out any clear facial features. They did not "believe" in the Fouke Monster, but they had no choice except to consider the possibility at that point. The shape, the size, and the way it moved ruled out most rational possibilities. Unless it was someone in a suit willing to sit in the rainy darkness and risk life and limb to run out in front of passing cars, there seemed to be no other explanation.

FOUKE FACTS: Michael and Liz Rowton were both non-believers when it came to the Fouke Monster. Liz had been employed at the Monster Mart convenience store for more than seven years, so she had heard more stories from locals and tourists than most anyone in Fouke, but even this did not convince her that it might be a real flesh and blood animal. However, after the incident, her mind was changed.

Source: Lyle Blackburn (personal interview)

May 2011 - Genoa

On May 5, 2011, an unnamed couple was driving to Genoa (about nine miles from Fouke) at around 7:30 p.m. As they drove down an old county road, they saw some sort of bipedal creature jump from the thick brush and run across the road in plain sight. It quickly disappeared into the woods, running in the direction of Old Bitty Lake. The couple described it as being about six feet tall with very stout legs. It was covered in reddish-brown hair that appeared to have "dirt and debris stuck to it." The husband promptly stopped the vehicle, at which time the couple could smell a rancid stench coming through the car's open window. The man was apparently an experienced outdoorsman who knew the woods and swamps of Arkansas well. The incident left him shaken.

Source: Lon Strickler

September 2011 - Fouke

Heather Owen, a Genoa resident, had gone to a friend's house in Fouke on the evening of September 28, 2011, to study for one of her college classes. At around 10:00 p.m., Owen began to hear a dog barking intensely somewhere outside the home. When Owen pointed it out, her friend told her it was their family pet and was probably making a fuss to come inside. Owen was struck by the particular nature of the barking.

"It sounded like the dog was very much distraught and was trying to alert the owner of some kind of danger," she told me. "But I dismissed the disturbance, since my friend didn't seem alarmed."

The intense barking continued for approximately forty-five minutes until it finally stopped. By midnight the girls were tired, so Owen packed up, said goodbye, and headed out into the night. It was clear and pleasant with a sliver of waxing moon overhead. It was also unusually quiet.

Owen got in her vehicle and started it up. She then rolled down the windows, opened the sunroof, and begin to navigate the narrow county roads. As she topped a hill, she spotted a figure standing beside a hay bale in the open field to her left. It appeared to be a human-like form, although it was unusually tall and bulky.

"My lights were on bright, and there was no mistaking it for what it was," she stated. "It was standing up on two feet facing towards me."

As Owen continued at a slow speed, the figure suddenly slouched forward and ran across the road with huge strides. It was so sudden that Owen slammed on her brakes for fear of hitting it. When it reached the opposite side of the road, it leapt over a drainage ditch and disappeared into the darkness beyond. The creature was muscular and covered in dark hair. In the moments before it ran, it turned sideways, giving Owen a profile view. She could see that "its shoulders looked massive, and its thighs were big."

Owen was so terrified by the event she immediately rolled up the windows, locked the doors, and closed the sunroof. She then drove a short way down the dark road and called her friend to ask if there had been reports of anything strange in the area lately. After a short conversation, she hung up and called her mother. By now she was shaking and driving as fast as she could toward the main road. She breathed intensely as she told her mother of the incident.

The following day, Heather and her mother came back to the area to look for evidence of the creature's passage but could only find an area of matted grass where it had presumably run.

FOUKE FACTS: This was the first new sighting report I received after the release of my first book, *The Beast of Boggy Creek: The True Story of the Fouke Monster*. Heather's encounter was later dramatized on the "Fouke Monster" episode of the television show *Monsters and Mysteries in America*, which also features an interview with me. I investigated the area where Heather claimed the creature crossed the road and concluded it would have been nearly impossible for a person to have navigated over a small ditch and jump a partially obscured, barbed-wire fence in the dark without getting caught up.

Source: Lyle Blackburn (personal interview)

February 2012 - Fouke at Fourmile Creek

In February 2012, at approximately 4:00 a.m., a woman was driving along a deserted county road near Fourmile Creek northwest of Fouke when she observed a hairy, bipedal animal run across the road and jump a fence before disappearing into the darkness. The woman (who requested to remain anonymous) is a longtime Fouke resident who is very familiar with the area's backroads.

Source: John Attaway

November 2012 - Fouke at Fourmile Creek

In November 2012, the woman who observed the strange, bipedal creature in February saw it again in the same, early morning time frame. This time, it appeared to be crouching alongside the road. She quickly accelerated and left the area. (See previous entry.)

Source: John Attaway

2012 - Fouke

While driving along a road south of Fouke near McKinney Bayou, a witness observed a large, hairy creature run across the road on two legs. It moved swiftly and disappeared into a line of thick woods.

Source: Denny Roberts

January 2013 - Carter Lake (Mercer Bayou)

In January 2013, Doyle Holmes—who had a possible encounter in 2004—was gathering firewood near Carter Lake at the lower end of Mercer Bayou when he heard an unusual moaning cry. Upon investigating, Holmes was stunned to find a strange animal standing in a clearing. The animal—which appeared to be a juvenile Sasquatch—was covered in dark hair and stood approximately four feet in height. When it saw Holmes, the creature bolted toward the bayou, running on two legs.

Holmes pursued the creature but lost sight of it when it waded into the murky water and disappeared behind a thick row of cypress trees. He tried to follow it into the water, but it was icy, and he had to abandon the foot search.

Holmes ran to his car and sped back to his house a short distance away. He loaded up his canoe, got his wife, and hurried back down to the area where he'd seen the creature. By the time Holmes got back to the site and launched the boat, however, he couldn't find the juvenile. Only after a short period did he hear its cry again, this time from the opposite bank of the small lake (which connects to the Mercer Bayou channel). He paddled across, but darkness was falling and visibility was becoming difficult. As the sun set, Holmes could hear splashing in the swampy waters nearby, sounding as though something very large and bipedal was making its way toward the juvenile's cry. He then heard a series of loud, bone-chilling whoops. At that point he grew frightened and returned to his truck.

FOUKE FACTS: Doyle Holmes, who has lived in the area since childhood, had a possible sighting back in April 2004 and found a set of strange footprints later that November. (See entry *April 2004 – Carter Lake*.)

Source: Lyle Blackburn (personal interview)

April 7, 2013 - Jonesville

In 2013, several colleagues and I were invited to participate in a television show that featured a Bigfoot theme. The show was *Shipping Wars*, which ran for seven seasons on the A&E network. In this episode, one of the truck driver cast members was transporting the legendary "Minnesota Iceman" from a location in

Minnesota to the Museum of the Weird in Austin, Texas.[iii] Since the Iceman has ties to Bigfoot history, the producers decided the driver should stop off in Fouke for an overnight excursion into the woods near Boggy Creek.

Present with me were Museum of the Weird owner, Steve Busti; Bigfoot investigators Ken Gerhard and Chris Buntenbah; Fouke local, John Attaway; and the truck driver. A small camera crew was there to capture the adventure on film. Our objective was to take the driver on an evening exploration in search of the famed creature.

We met at the Monster Mart on the afternoon of April 7 and then proceeded to the filming location. I chose an area in Jonesville near Boggy Creek and the Sulphur River. It was in prime Fouke Monster territory and close to the locations of several credible encounters. The crew set up, and we began filming just before sunset.

During the shoot, camera operator William Zilliox was filming B-roll scenery shots in a thick section of the woods when he heard something running through the brush. He was using the camera's night vision feature to capture the ambiance of the dark surroundings. When he focused it in the direction of the sound, he saw what looked like a very large person running toward him at a distance of approximately fifty yards. It would not have been unusual, except the figure was moving at a high rate of speed through very thick brush—something that would be very difficult for a person. The entity ran toward Zilliox at a bit of an angle and then ran off without ever stopping.

"Believe it or not, I actually filmed it!" Zilliox told me.

After the incident, the crew did not seem quite as skeptical as

---

iii The Minnesota Iceman was an exhibit shown during the late 1960s and early 1970s at carnivals and fairs around the United States and Canada. The exhibit consisted of an alleged Bigfoot-like creature encased in a solid block of ice. The contents of the exhibit were purchased by Steve Busti in 2013 and are now on display at his Museum of the Weird in Austin.

they did before. It was the nature of the Fouke woods to sway one's opinion after only a short period of exploration into its terrain.

The possibility of misidentification or hoax cannot be ruled out in this case. Someone might have overheard us at the Monster Mart and decided to discretely follow the entourage into Jonesville for a prank. But it seems unlikely, since we were filming at a location on private property. Not to mention, they would not have been able to access the location easily without passing by us. It was not one of the crew members, either, as they were all accounted for at the time. The other aspect was the runner's speed and agility while navigating through very thick brush. A large person could not have accomplished that feat in full view of the camera.

"I recall getting cut really bad if I ever tried to walk outside of the path you guys cleared," Zilliox recalled. "The speed at which this 'person' was running through the brush was very impressive."

Later that night while we were sitting in the woods, Ken played a wounded animal call in an attempt to elicit a response from any potential creatures. After a few moments, something suddenly bolted into the woods a mere twenty yards away. It sounded very large and made considerable noise as it ran into the brush. Whatever it was had been lingering very close to our group when it decided to run off.

In the end, Zilliox could not be certain the large, humanoid figure he saw was the Fouke Monster, but he could not rule it out either. Surprisingly, the network did not end up using the footage in the final cut of the episode! Why they wouldn't include something like that is a total mystery. Perhaps somewhere in the vast digital film archives of the production company lies the only footage of the legendary Fouke creature ever captured. We can only hope someday it will be released for further analysis.

FOUKE FACTS: The location of this incident was very close to the pond where Terry Sutton had an incredible sighting in

1982. (See entry *February 20, 1982 – Jonesville.*)

Source: Lyle Blackburn (personal interview)

November 25, 2014 - Sulphur River

On the morning of Tuesday, November 25, 2014, a woman living near the Sulphur River west of Fouke was driving along a small county road north from her home at around 10:00 a.m. She was on her way to see her mother at the hospital and realized she had forgotten something. She slowed down and turned around on the narrow county road. As she began to head back south, she was startled by something standing in the middle of the road. At first she thought it was a kid dressed in a Halloween costume, but as she focused on the figure, she realized it was some sort of hairy animal, one that walked on two legs.

The creature had apparently come out of the thick patch of woods on her left and was crossing the road where her car had been moments before. Now that she had turned around, it paused as if caught in the act. The creature stood fully upright with an estimated height of five feet. It was covered in reddish-brown hair except for the face, which had dark, leathery skin and particularly piercing eyes. She could see the wispy hair on its arms—about four inches long and waving in the gentle morning breeze. It gazed at the woman for a few seconds before it turned and ran back into the woods.

Completely unnerved, the woman sped home, grabbed what she had forgotten, and drove back up the road until she reached a convenience store. She did not see the creature again but was still shaking so much she decided to stop and pick up a soda, hoping to calm her nerves. As luck would have it, she struck up a conversation with the owner, who happened to be my friend Denny Roberts, who also owns the Monster Mart in Fouke. She told him about the encounter, and he assured her she was not the only one to have seen something like that in the Sulphur River area. He suggested she talk with me, and she agreed to an interview. She did not want any publicity, fearing her neighbors might think she'd "gone crazy," so I promised to keep her name confidential.

A month later we met at the convenience store, where she reiterated the story to me and my late research partner Tom Shirley. As she spoke, we could sense the emotion in her voice. I watched the earnest expression in her eyes. It was apparent feelings of fear and bewilderment still lingered.

"It scared me to death," she told us. "I was shaking for days, and I'm still wondering if I really saw that."

She was puzzled that its apparent height of five feet did not equal the towering Bigfoot stature she had heard about. I explained it's only logical that if these creatures are real, then naturally there would be younger ones who haven't reached full maturity, not to mention I had heard plenty of other witness reports where the creatures were of heights that varied from four to eight feet. Her description was not out of the ordinary and, in fact, quite common in the attributes of its reddish-brown hair and darker facial skin.

I asked her if there was any possibility it could have been a person in a costume, perhaps trying to scare her.

"At first I thought it was a kid in a costume, but the more I looked at it, I could see it wasn't," she explained. "And when it was running, it didn't look like a costume; it looked like a real animal."

There are not many homes in the area, and the place where the creature presumably came out of the woods is very thick. I talked to the nearest homeowner, who assured me no kids would be out there running around in a costume. He was the only one with kids of that age, and they were at school. In fact, most kids would have been in school. This was the Tuesday before Thanksgiving, a regular school day.

FOUKE FACTS: The location of this sighting is along the Sulphur River in Texas, approximately eleven miles west of

Fouke. The Sulphur River, which runs through Fouke, originates in Texas near the town of Commerce. There is a long history of Sasquatch sightings around the Sulphur River on the Texas side as well. In 1969 and 1978, there were a rash of encounters near Commerce. The same creature (or creatures) seen around Fouke could have also been responsible for these sightings, since they seem to travel up and down the network of creeks and rivers.

Source: Lyle Blackburn (personal interview)

The road where a woman saw a strange creature on Nov. 25, 2014
(Photo by Lyle Blackburn)

May 15, 2016 - Fouke

In the early morning hours of May 15, 2016, Traci Sanders was driving south on Highway 71 just north of Fouke when she noticed something standing near the road. It was big and standing upright. It looked peculiar with very long arms. A few seconds later, it darted across the road, moving swiftly on two legs with long strides. It ran into the woods on the other side and disappeared from sight.

Sanders was delivering newspapers at the time, so she had her windows down. The incident startled her so much, she stopped the car and sat there a moment trying to process what she had just seen. As she sat there, she could smell a foul odor beginning to waft through the air. She surmised it had been left by the creature.

Sanders eventually regained her composure and continued on her route. A few minutes later as she traveled on a county road directly across (as the crow files) from where she saw the strange animal, she noticed the dogs were visibly agitated.

"There's houses back there, and there's usually dogs just laying around on the street and in the driveways; you couldn't stir them with a stick," Sanders explained. "But that morning, those dogs were stirred up and hair bristling on their back. Something had spooked those dogs."

FOUKE FACTS: The location where Sanders saw the thing run across the road is just south of where the old "Ford House" was located. (See entry *April 28 through May 3, 1971*.)

Source: Lyle Blackburn (personal interview)

February 18, 2017 - Sulphur River WMA

In the winter of 2017, Jim Whitehead and David Moomey were driving down a dirt road in the Sulphur River Wildlife Management Area at around 3:00 p.m. It was overcast, and they were scouting locations for a potential research outing. When they came to an intersection with a narrow side road, they looked in that direction. According to Whitehead, they both saw a large, upright figure standing in the middle of the road. It quickly darted into the woods as they hit the brakes.

"It was probably around seven feet tall and had reddish hair, like an Irish Setter," Whitehead told me. "The hair on the head and upper chest was much darker, either a dark brown or a black."

Whitehead and Moomey got out of the car and went to the location where the thing had been standing. They found a small trail leading in the woods. In the dirt, they could see faint impressions, which appeared to be footprints.

"We then decided to head out and get audio recorders, and that's when we caught movement a second time," Whitehead continued. "We didn't get a good look at whatever that was, but the initial sighting I did."

Whitehead tried to take a photo of the figure as it ran through the woods; however, it was obscured by the thick brush. The resulting image was unclear and inconclusive. They returned to the area later that night and recorded some strange vocalizations but never saw the creature again.

Source: Jim Whitehead

The legendary Boggy Creek
(Photo by Lyle Blackburn)

May 5, 2017 - Fouke at Boggy Creek

On May 5, 2017, Bruce and Pam Jennings were driving on Interstate Highway 49 south of Fouke in the late afternoon. As they crossed the Boggy Creek bridge, Pam saw what looked like a huge, hairy figure standing near the tree line on the northbound side of the road. She was only able to see it for a few moments due to the speed of the vehicle.

Source: Lyle Blackburn (personal interview)

October 2017 - Fouke

In the fall of 2017, truck driver Don Martin was driving south on Interstate Highway 49 around noon. As he neared the Highway 71 exit, he saw a large, hairy figure crouching on two legs in the pipeline between a fence and a deer stand.

Source: Lyle Blackburn (personal interview)

October 14, 2018 - Fouke

On the evening of October 14, 2018, at approximately 7:00 p.m., Wendy Rathburn and Lana Jones were driving on Highway 71 south of Fouke when they saw a large, bulky figure run across the road in four huge strides. It ran on two legs and continued to run down the middle of another road that is perpendicular to the highway. The startled women initially passed by the crossroad but decided to stop and turn around. When they turned on the road where the thing had run, it was already gone. The two women were confident it was some kind of animal, not a person in a costume.

Source: Lyle Blackburn (personal interview)

February 2019 - Fouke

A man was driving on a county road south of Fouke after dark when he noticed red eyeshine in the woods to his right. As he approached, he could make out the form of a large, humanoid figure standing flush with the line of trees. It turned its head as he slowed down and passed by, apparently watching the car. The figure looked to be six or seven feet tall with a muscular form and hair covering its body. The driver (who requested to remain anonymous), watched it a few more seconds until it turned and slipped into the shadows. The man was too frightened to stop and investigate further.

FOUKE FACTS: The location of this sighting is close to the area known as Thornton Wells, where many strange incidents have occurred over the years including sightings, strange howls, and wood knocks.

Source: Lyle Blackburn (personal interview)

December 7, 2019 - Mercer Bayou

On the night of December 7, 2019, Dustin Clark and several friends were scouting a wooded area at the north end of Mercer Bayou when Clark decided to walk ahead by himself. The moon was bright, which provided enough ambient light to see into the woods without having to turn on the intrusive beam of his headlamp. After he was away from the group, Clark knelt down and scanned the dark road ahead looking for any signs of nocturnal wildlife. He saw something move. It was the silhouette of large figure walking between two trees to his left.

"What caught my eye was actually the moonlight; it was glaring off the hair on the back of the head, the shoulder, and the back of the arm as it was moving left to right," Clark explained. "When I looked over, I could see the shape go across."

The shape disappeared behind some trees as Clark grappled

with the possibilities. "I was in disbelief, excited, and my adrenaline was pumping," he said.

Clark reacted quickly, calling to his friend Steven, who had a pair of night vision binoculars. Steven hurried to where Clark was standing, and they began scanning the trees with the binoculars, hoping to catch another glimpse of the figure. They watched for several minutes, but nothing moved.

"I'd almost given up when I looked over on the same side of the road—down in this gulley—and I saw more movement," Clark continued. "It went between some trees."

He raised the binoculars again and began scanning the area around the trees. After some work to focus them, Clark finally locked onto the figure again. In the green-white hue of the night vision, Clark could see part of its head, face, and shoulders as it peered around the trunk of a tree and looked at him with white eyeshine. He was shocked; so shocked, he momentarily pulled the binoculars away from his eyes. When both he and Steven looked again, the thing was no longer visible.

After some discussion, they decided to advance slowly toward the trees. When they got there, however, whatever Clark had seen was gone.

Source: Dustin Clark (published video account)

December 2019 - Fouke

The witness in this case—a man identified as 'JR'—owns a 400-acre farm in Miller County just west of Fouke. The farm contains a large field that sits adjacent to a wooded bottomland that is usually covered by water. JR often hunts the edges of the field, but rarely goes into the flooded area since deer and other game seem to avoid it.

One morning in December 2019, JR was hunting from a tree stand at the edge of the field when he began to smell a rotten odor. He figured it must have been from a decomposing cow he had placed at the far end of the field a few days prior. The cow had died of unknown causes, so JR used a tractor to drag it as far away from the hunting area as he could.

The hunter began scanning the area with his binoculars, looking for signs of deer. As he did, he caught sight of a dark figure at the end of a game trail about one hundred fifty yards away. He thought it might be a feral hog until it stood up on two legs. It appeared to be at least six feet tall and covered in long, matted, black hair. The thing appeared to be "muscular but not thick in the torso."

JR was aware of the Fouke Monster stories, but did not believe that it, nor any kind of Bigfoot, existed. His opinion was changing, however, as he studied the creature standing before him. It seemed to be observing his field as it stood in one spot "rocking side-to-side" for several minutes. It did not appear to notice JR, who was concealed in his tree stand. After several surreal minutes, the thing turned and walked toward the wooded bottomland and disappeared into the shadows.

Though he had heard several firsthand accounts by other Fouke residents, he was reluctant to share his own experience with the locals. Nonetheless, he is now "convinced that these creatures live on or near his property."

Source: Lon Strickler

December 2019 - Jonesville

A young witness claims to have seen a "monkey man" in the woods while sitting in her father's truck along one of the rural roads at night. The location is near the Sulphur River, where many sightings of the alleged Fouke Monster have been reported over the years.

Source: Lyle Blackburn (personal interview with the father)

4.

The Evidence

While the existence of the Fouke Monster has yet to be proven, the case does offer some possible physical evidence. This evidence consists primarily of footprint tracks discovered in and around Fouke that appear to have been made by an unidentified animal. In some instances, a plaster cast was made of the track(s), while in others we only have a story. This is not surprising, however, because not all individuals who run across a strange footprint in the woods have the means to cast them, or even the motivation. In cases where an encounter took place, many of the witnesses were simply too afraid to look for tracks.

Alleged photos of the creature have also surfaced on occasion, although the majority of these lack enough clarity to be conclusive. This is not to say they are not photos of the said creature, just that they would not be considered proof.

A lack of definitive proof doesn't mean the creature (or creatures) does not exist, of course, but in terms of science, more physical evidence will be required to conclusively add the Fouke Monster to the official list of Arkansas fauna.

The following sections provide information on some of the more prominent track discoveries as well as some of my own insights. (Photos are included for those in which permission was granted by the owner/photographer.)

Classic Tracks

Crabtree Lake - 1960s

Following the encounter reported by James Lynn Crabtree in 1965, his father, Smokey Crabtree, and others formed a search party to look for the creature. The creature thereafter would periodically come around the Crabtree home and wander through the nearby woods. On one occasion, Smokey found some strange tracks, which he would later compare to those discovered in Willie Smith's bean field (see entry below for *June 13, 1971*.)

Source: Smokey Crabtree

Ford House - May 1971

During the "Ford House" incidents of April/May 1971, several strange tracks were found. The first was discovered on the banks of a nearby creek. Bobby Ford and Corky Hill had gone there to fish on the afternoon of May 1. When they arrived, they immediately noticed a strange-looking footprint pressed into the mud along the bank. It was described as having only "three toes."

After Bobby Ford was "attacked" by the hairy creature that had been trying to get into their home, law officials combed the area for evidence. During the search, they found what the *Texarkana Gazette* newspaper described as "several strange tracks – that appeared to be left by something with three toes – and several scratch marks on the front porch that appeared to have been made by something with three claws." Unfortunately, no photos or castings were made of these tracks. (See entry *April 28 through May 2, 1971* for more details.)

FOUKE FACTS: This article, with its statement about a track with "three toes," is what initially established the idea that the Fouke Monster has a foot with three toes.

Source: *Texarkana Gazette*

Authorities on horseback search the "Ford House"
property on May 3, 1971
(Photo courtesy of the Northwest Arkansas Times)

Oats Road - June 6, 1971

On Sunday, June 6, Miller County Constable Paul Jewell and Deputy Constable Richard Haygood were investigating several reports of a "monster" seen near Oats and Washington Street in Texarkana when they discovered what appeared to be five unidentified animal tracks in the soft soil surrounding a fertilizer plant on North Oats Road. The prints, which were "shaped like dog tracks," measured four inches wide. They could not tell if the animal's foot had claws because of the nature of the soil. A freshly killed pigeon was discovered in the area by Jewell, who said he believed whatever kind of creature people were seeing was still in the area. The men staked out the fertilizer plant, but did not spot the animal.

Something like this would not normally make news, but in this case it did because of the dramatic Fouke Monster sightings making headlines at the time. If these footprints were similar to that of a dog, yet had no claws, then perhaps they were left by a large wildcat such as cougar. Either way, they were not described as having "three toes," nor were they likely to be the prints of a bipedal, ape-like creature.

Source: Texarkana Gazette

Willie Smith's Bean Field - June 13, 1971

On the morning of Sunday, June 13, 1971, Yother Kennedy was inspecting a freshly plowed soybean field located near the southern end of Boggy Creek when he found a series of mysterious footprints. The prints originated from the woods at one corner of the field and traveled about one hundred fifty yards before disappearing into the trees on the other side. The trackway appeared to have been made by a bipedal creature walking upright. According to an article in the *Texarkana Gazette*, the tracks measured thirteen and a half inches long by four and a half inches wide with a maximum stride of fifty-seven inches between them. The animal appeared to have three toes all about the same length. Another, smaller toe imprint was observed about five inches back from the big toe, but this digit only made a faint indention in the sandy soil.

Several law and game officials were called to the scene that morning, including Constable Ernest Walraven, Miller County Sheriff Leslie Greer, Deputy H.L. Phillips, and game warden, Carl Gaylon. Walraven, who had previously investigated the Ford incidents, told reporters: "At first I didn't think too much of the sightings but now I do. I have never seen tracks like this and I have been in the woods all my life." Gaylon and Greer had never seen animal tracks like those before, so they could not make a judgment as to whether they were authentic, only that they were indeed mysterious.

"MONSTER" TRACKS FOUND — Strange tracks were found late Sunday in a freshly plowed field three miles southeast of Fouke, Ark. The tracks measured 13 and a half inches long and had three toes, all the same size and all about two inches long. The track was four and a half inches wide at the front and three inches at the heel. The strange tracks were found in an area where several strange noises have been heard in the past few weeks. (Staff Photo)

One of the tracks found in Willie Smith's bean field on June 13, 1971
(Courtesy of the Texarkana Gazette)

Smokey Crabtree and Willie Smith (who owned the land) also converged on the scene. Smokey's son had seen the alleged creature several years before, so he was interested in what evidence the tracks may offer. Smith informed the press that he and his family had seen these type of tracks in the area many times in the past. He theorized that the creature must live and roam in the vicinity of the creeks, which more or less spread out in a ring around Fouke. "Every time it has been seen around here, it has always been near one of the creeks," he told reporters.

Word of the track find eventually spread around town, and more of the locals came down to the field to see for themselves. Rickie Roberts, whose father served as mayor from 1978-1991, was one such person. Like the others, Roberts didn't know what to make of the tracks, but he was definitely impressed by the distance between them. In a series of personal interviews I had with

Roberts, he told me: "If the tracks were a hoax, they would have been very hard to fake. It would not have been easy for a person to get that much distance between each one."

Rickie's mother, Jane Roberts, made a cast of one of the footprints using plaster of Paris. Fouke officials had very little experience in casting at the time, so Robert's mother, skilled with arts and crafts, assisted them. Smokey Crabtree was said to have literally cut one from the surrounding soil and placed it in a box.

Journalist Jim Powell and radio personality Dave Hall represented the press that day. They had both been present at the Ford investigation, so naturally they were interested by the strange find. Powell was not as convinced as Walraven that the tracks were those of a real animal or even an unknown creature. "I noticed that it stepped over the plants," he told me during a phone conversation. "I've never seen an animal that didn't step on plants as it crossed a field. It just didn't seem right." This was puzzling. Those present agreed that whoever had made the tracks had been reluctant to step on any of the young bean plants.

Regardless, there was no denying that *something* had made strange tracks in the soil, whether it was a strange animal or just a clever hoaxer. Since there was no solid evidence pointing either way, it was simply news, and Powell reported it that way. The resulting story appeared in the June 15 edition of the *Texarkana Gazette*, taking up the better part of a page that featured a large photo of a single track and the headline: "Monster Tracks Found."

The castings made from these tracks were eventually displayed in Willie Smith's gas station and later at the Boggy Creek Café. In a tragic turn of events, the casts were destroyed when the Boggy Creek Café caught fire in the late 1970s.

FOUKE FACTS: The bean field track discovery was reenacted in *The Legend of Boggy Creek*. Radio news reporter Dave Hall can be seen playing himself in the scene.

Sources: *Texarkana Gazette*, Lyle Blackburn (personal interviews)

*Fouke Mayor Virgil Roberts holds an original
track casting from the bean field
(Courtesy of Rickie Roberts)*

Zorn Track - 1973

Another vintage track cast is owned by Tom Zorn, who grew up in Fouke and has spent much of his life researching the Fouke Monster. The track was found near Boggy Creek in 1973 and cast by Doris L. Brown. It measures roughly fifteen inches in length and six and a half inches wide at the ball. The cast is somewhat rough and does not show a very clear indication of the toe count, although it does look very similar to the tracks found in Willie Smith's bean field.

Zorn's track is on display at the Monster Mart in Fouke. The Monster Mart has a small museum area where various tracks, memorabilia, and other items related to the Fouke Monster are displayed.

Scoggins Farm - November 1973

On the morning of November 25, 1973, Orville Scoggins observed a black-haired, four-foot tall creature walk across a field behind his home. The animal was walking upright on two legs the entire time. Scoggins, Constable Red Walraven, and two other men searched the area where the creature had been sighted and found a line of tracks left in the soil. The tracks measured five and a half inches in diameter and were spaced forty inches apart. The men followed the tracks for nearly an eighth of a mile before the trail finally disappeared into the woods.

These tracks were shorter than the thirteen-inch tracks found in Willie Smith's field, but Constable Walraven noted: "These were the same tracks that were found the first time the monster was sighted." (Presumably, this meant they had three toes like those found at the Ford house.)

Source: *Texarkana Gazette*

Modern Tracks

Sulphur River - August 2003

In August 2003, two men claimed to have found several tracks near one of the Sulphur River boat ramps. They said the footprints bore a striking resemblance to human tracks, yet they were odd because some were disproportionately wide. They took some measurements to determine that one of the best tracks was twelve inches long and five to six inches wide. Another one measured fourteen inches in length. Certainly not out of human range, but if they weren't obviously human, then what were they?

Source: Gulf Coast Bigfoot Research Organization

Carter Lake - November 2004

A five-toed footprint was cast by Doyle Holmes in November 2004. The track, which represents the imprint of a left foot, measures fifteen inches long by eight and a half inches wide at the toes and five and a half inches wide at the ball. The photo here does not do it justice, but upon examining it in person, it clearly has five distinct toe impressions. It also appears to have some kind of growth or bunion protruding from under the largest toe, which was consistent with all the footprints found in the trackway.

Whatever or whoever created the tracks was not spotted at the time, but the circumstances surrounding their discovery suggest they were not likely to be a hoax. I interviewed Mr. Holmes at length and also spoke to his son, Nathan, who initially spotted the tracks, and I found them to be straightforward and sincere about their story.

The discovery of the tracks took place a day or two after Thanksgiving in 2004 while Holmes and his son were hog hunting in an area the locals call "Carter Lake" (located at the southern end of Mercer Bayou). They had taken a boat so they could travel more easily through the area, which is extremely swampy. The duo had paddled a good distance down Carter Lake when they got out to look for signs of hogs. A short time later they came up on a large group of hogs and began to follow them along the bank near the water. As Nathan was looking for traces of hog tracks trying to determine which way they had gone, he noticed a strange set of footprints leading out of the water toward a berry patch nearby. The tracks registered clearly in the moist soil, numbering about ten total, before they disappeared into vegetation. These looked very peculiar, so Nathan called his father over to have a look. Doyle inspected the tracks and was shocked at the size. They appeared human-like, with five toes, but they were much larger and had an oddly shaped foot.

The tracks were fairly fresh, so they followed them into the berry patch until they could no longer be seen. Without a way to cast the impressions, Doyle decided to mark the spot and return later. He and Nathan headed out, wondering just what kind of animal had made the tracks. Inevitably, the Fouke Monster came to mind. Two days later, Doyle returned with cement, intent on preserving the tracks. Unfortunately, many of them had begun to erode, and the best track had been partially stepped on a by a hog, but still he was able to get one good sample.

The track cast by Doyle Holmes in November 2004
(Photo by Lyle Blackburn)

Long Slough - January 2015

On the night of January 23, 2015, Tom Shirley and I were walking on a dirt trail through a heavily wooded area near Long Slough west of Fouke when we found what appeared to be a classic three- or four-toed track. The impression had been left in a muddy puddle. It had been raining off and on that week, and puddles dotted the low points along the trail.

It was after midnight, and we were in an area far from the road and not accessible by any means aside from foot or four-wheeler. The flashlight reflected sharply off the water, but nonetheless we could see what definitely looked like a long foot impression with three or perhaps four toes. The impression was perpendicular to the trail, as if whatever had stepped there was crossing as it walked through the woods. We looked for additional tracks but did not find any. This was not surprising. Leaves and pine straw covered the ground on either side of the thin ruts of the trail, so only a footstep in the mud would have registered a track.

We did not have any casting material with us, so we returned the following day with fellow researcher, Bryan Impey, and attempted to cast it. The track was almost completely submerged in an inch of water, so we removed as much water as we could without disturbing the track's integrity, and then poured in a Hydrocal mixture. We waited for a few hours, but due to the cold, wet conditions of the weather and substrate, the plaster was simply not setting up properly. At that point we decided to leave it and hope that by the next day it would harden enough to safely extract it. Tom and I had to leave the next day, but Bryan volunteered to retrieve it. This was a huge favor, since the area was remote, lonely, and really quite creepy, not to mention we had found what appeared to be a monster track!

Bryan retrieved the cast the following day, but the result was disappointing. It had hardened, but it was not very solid, so parts broke off. And because the impression was made in wet, fragile mud, it simply did not capture the detail we had seen in person. While there is certainly no way of knowing whether the legendary Fouke Monster made the footprint or if it was simply an illusion created by some coincidentally perfect conditions, we believe that perhaps we had come across something rare and quite extraordinary.

Photo of the possible track found by
the author and Tom Shirley in 2015
(Photo by Lyle Blackburn)

Sulphur River - March 2019

Around March 18, 2019, Tammy Hinds and Kaitlin Jones were walking along the bank of the Sulphur River near the boat ramp south of Fouke when they noticed some small but curious tracks. Thinking they might have something to do with the Fouke Monster, they called their uncle, Rickie Roberts, and asked him to take a look.

When Roberts arrived, he was inspecting the small tracks when he spotted some larger tracks coming from the woods and ending at the water. It had been raining off and on that month, so the soil was moist and muddy all around the river. The tracks were long and narrow and showed what looked to be marks from four or five toes, although the toe marks did not register very cleanly because whatever left the tracks appeared to have been running when they were made. They measured approximately fifteen inches in length by five inches wide. The track maker may have been chasing a deer, judging by some deer hoof impressions that ran in the same direction as the unidentified tracks. It looked as though the deer had possibly been chased into the water or grabbed just prior to hitting the water because its tracks also ended at the bank. (The bank drops off drastically at this spot, so it was an unlikely place for a deer to approach the water if it were merely trying to get a drink.)

A week after the tracks were found, I went to Fouke and personally inspected them. It had rained once since their discovery, causing some erosion, but most of the tracks were still visible. They came from the woods, progressed down an incline across some mud, and ended at the water's edge. There were about seven visible tracks spanning a distance of approximately thirty yards. The last one was essentially a slide mark leading down to the water. They seemed natural and did not appear to have been manufactured.

Because of the erosion, it was hard to see the toe marks at that point, but I could still see where they had presumably pushed up mud at the tips. Perhaps if the maker had not been running, it would have been the perfect conditions for registering a pristine footprint. As such, we could not be certain what had truly made the tracks.

FOUKE FACTS: The Sulphur River is a definite hotspot for finding tracks, and this stands to reason. Not only is the muddy bank conducive for leaving tracks, but there have been a number of creature sightings up and down the river throughout the years.

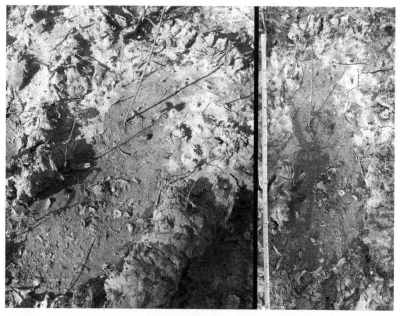

Odd tracks found on the banks of the Sulphur River in March 2019
(Photos by Lyle Blackburn)

A Question of Three Toes

The fact that many of the suspected Fouke Monster tracks exhibit only three toes raises a number of complex questions regarding not only the nature of the creature but the authenticity of the case itself. While there have been some "Bigfoot" tracks found elsewhere across the United States that possess this three-toed configuration, and even a four-toed configuration, in general, a Sasquatch is theorized to have five toes, which would be typical of any other higher primate, whether extinct or living in the world today. If the Fouke Monster is presumed to be one of these creatures, and it does have three toes, this may suggest it is a species separate from any proposed population of Sasquatch creatures that may exist in the countryside. Understandably, this is something of a problem when trying to simplify the case for the Fouke Monster, since it implies the creature might not even be a logical evolution of a primate—albeit a yet-to-be-discovered one.

The issue is even more complicated because some of the unidentified tracks found around Fouke (primarily in modern times) have more than three toes. So in the end, does the creature have three toes, four toes, five toes, or could some of these footprints be nothing more than misidentifications or hoaxes? Some have suggested the trackway found in Willie Smith's bean field was an intentional hoax, yet even so it would have been very hard to create the tracks. Some people who saw the tracks in person had doubts as to their authenticity. "I noticed that it stepped over the plants," reporter Jim Powell recalled. To him, it seemed a bit too convenient that the animal would have avoided stepping on any of the soybean plants.

Some were not so quick to jump to conclusions either way. Rickie Roberts noted the long stride measurements and the sheer number of tracks. "It would have been really hard to fake those," he told me, remembering his first impression when he saw the tracks in person as a teenager. Carl Gaylon, the game warden who examined the tracks at the time, could not make a definite ruling either, only that he had never seen tracks like that before. Constable Walraven, who was dubious about the "monster" at first, seemed swayed by the new footprint evidence.

Smokey Crabtree weighed in on the matter by telling the *Texarkana Gazette* that "the tracks found in the area in 1963 looked like the same print." And Tom Shirley and I found a track much more recently that appeared to have three toes. I'm absolutely sure it was not something planted by a hoaxer due to the remote and random location where we found it.

Some experts theorize that because of a limited population, the three-toed foot represents some type of congenital deformation caused by inbreeding in some individuals. An animal like this would surely have a limited population. However, this type of manifestation usually results in a more deformed looking foot all around, which is not the case here. The tracks found in the bean field, for example, show the foot to be fairly uniform except for the fact it has three toes.

The question of the Fouke Monster's foot anatomy, if the creature does exist, is one that has puzzled researchers for many years. And until we have further proof, it is a question that will continue to linger like the memory of a startling encounter with a creature that is entirely unknown.

5.

Land of the
Legend

Wild Country

The backdrop for these incredible encounters is a country that is as wild as the ostensible beast itself. The town of Fouke is located a mere twenty minutes south of the metropolitan city of Texarkana, yet it sits in a region streaked with tracts of thick forestry and saturated with miles of swampy bottomlands. The Sulphur River Wildlife Management Area—which encompasses many of the sighting locations—is nearly twenty thousand acres unto itself. When we add up the surrounding acreage of additional woods, farms, and bayous, the land of the legend seems truly vast even by today's standards. And that is only logical, considering a creature such as the Fouke Monster would require a rich habitat where it could thrive in relative obscurity away from the reaching hands of civilization.

If you take a drive down the backroads of Fouke, it is easier to understand why this mystery has endured and why it would be hard to locate a reclusive creature (or more logically, a small population of these creatures) in this expanse. Each mile along these old country roads unfolds acre after acre of riparian, hardwood bottomlands where something could potentially survive for decades while rarely being spotted. The woods, especially in the spring and summer months, are so dense it is hard to penetrate very far with the naked eye. The dark shadows that gather beyond their edges create an astounding number of pockets where anything can hide. In fact, if the creature merely stood still as your car passed by, you would hardly notice its portentous presence lurking just a few scant feet inside the tree line.

In terms of geography, the vast woodlands and swamps of the Sulphur River Bottoms are part of the greater Red River Basin, which flows from the border of Oklahoma and Texas through Arkansas on its way toward the Mississippi River. This great network of waterways provides some of the best habitat for supporting natural wildlife in the southern states area, and perhaps not surprisingly, Fouke sits almost smack dab in the middle of the richest concentration of forestland in the four-state region of Arkansas, Louisiana, Oklahoma, and Texas. By combining the total forestland at the intersection of these four states—which is only miles from Fouke—we arrive at a staggering sixty-five million acres, or 100,000 square miles.

"He always travels the creeks." So say the locals. And certainly there are plenty of muddy tributaries leading from the deep reaches of the Arkansas bottomlands to the edges of civilization that the alleged creature could follow. In fact, if we were to go looking for such a thing as a "Southern Sasquatch," this would be a logical place to start. The area is not only a marshy bottomland but a densely forested region that has all the necessary ingredients to host an animal like the one reportedly seen near Fouke.

Like much of rural America, the area has seen change and deforestation over the last decade, yet its core still survives in the deeper reaches of the Sulphur Basin and Mercer Bayou where Boggy Creek empties into the vast shadows. This is a rugged place that cannot be easily developed or erased, as evidenced by the substantial amount of forestry still remaining. Though the jaws of civilization may be closing in, the land of the legend still beats with the heart of a wild country; a wild country that seems intent on protecting its venerable secrets.

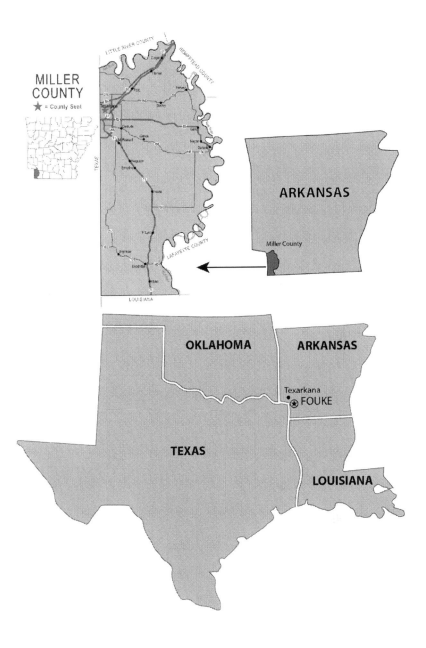

Monster Mart

When I started researching the case of the Fouke Monster over a decade ago, I visited a curious establishment in Fouke called the Monster Mart. In those days, the Monster Mart was an unassuming little convenience store that only hinted at the town's big legend. The exterior of the store did have a small mural of the creature, but the inside merely offered a cheerless curio case and a few old newspaper clippings tacked to bulletin board near the front door. It was better than nothing, but all in all it was a rather disappointing display of memorabilia and crude merchandise that, to me, seemed unworthy of the town's intriguing history.

However, since the release of my book, *The Beast of Boggy Creek,* in 2012, there have been some major changes that have elevated the historical recognition of the legend and the curb appeal of the Monster Mart itself.

One reason for the transformation is due to the current owners, the Roberts family. Shortly after my first visit, the store was purchased by Denny Roberts. Roberts grew up in Fouke and has a deep respect for the historical aspect of the legend. It was his intention to improve the Monster Mart and make it a place where visitors could find information about the creature, view historic items, and of course, find a few quality souvenirs that folks could take home with them.

Another reason for the transformation is the visitors themselves (perhaps yourself). There's not a day that goes by in which at least someone from out of town—even from other countries—stops into the Monster Mart to ask about the creature. It is this steady stream of fascinated people that Denny felt deserved something better.

Moving toward this goal, the Roberts family (it's a true family operation) has transformed the inside *and* outside of the store. Whereas once visitors could only find a small curio case and yellowed clippings on a corkboard, there is now a room dedicated to the monstrous legend. The room features a huge mural of the creature (great for photo ops), framed newspaper articles, movie posters, and life-sized, museum-quality replicas. Framed photos of important locations can also be found hanging throughout the store. The merchandise, as well, has gone from one crude t-shirt design and a few postcards to an array of cool Fouke Monster items including mugs, keychains, hand-made dolls, vials of Boggy Creek "Swamp Water," posters, several t-shirts, and of course, books. This may seem like a plan to capitalize on the legend, and in some ways it is since it is part of the Roberts' source of income, but it is done out of respect and in response to all the travelers that have dropped by and asked for souvenirs. The money brought in by these sales has also helped fund more improvements, one of these being the huge "Monster Mart" sign on top of the building. Not only does the sign feature the store name in big, bold letters, it boasts a sculpture of an enormous Bigfoot creature rising up from the rooftop! Combine this with the swampy, cypress tree façade of the store front, and the Monster Mart is no longer a place that merely hints at a big legend—it's a legend unto itself.

Of course, some may prefer that the legend remain quiet. And that's their privilege. But as a lifelong fan of *The Legend of Boggy Creek*, I can't help but to be thrilled.

Visit the Fouke Monster Mart at:

104 Highway 71
Fouke, Arkansas 71837

Exterior view of the Fouke Monster Mart
(Photo by Lyle Blackburn)

A "Fouke Monster family" on display inside the Monster Mart
(Photo by Lyle Blackburn)

Conclusion

A few months before I settled in to write this book, my friend Jerry Hestand and I decided to make a spontaneous trip to Fouke. We hadn't been there for a while, so we were looking forward to catching up with friends and hiking the woods before the weather turned frosty. As we often did, we spent a good portion of the day hanging out at the Monster Mart and dropping by various friends' homes to visit. It's always great to see everyone, get the latest info on river levels and game reports, and of course, find out if anyone had reported a sighting of the creature.

During the course of our visit, we learned of a secondhand sighting that had occurred near the Sulphur River. The sighting wasn't too dramatic, but that didn't stop us from driving to the spot to have a look around. We're familiar with the county roads and landmarks at this point, so it was not hard to find, even without the witness showing us. We noted the proximity of the road to the river and concluded it would be a likely place for a creature to cross if it were passing through that particular patch of woods.

The sighting location is close to the cemetery where our late friend Smokey Crabtree is buried, so we decided to head over and pay our respects before we finally headed to the woods. The weather that day was bipolar, alternating between sunny skies and gray overcast. A chance of rain was in the forecast, but so far the ashen clouds were only an idle threat. Quick storms are common to the area, so we weren't too worried that it would spoil our chance for an evening excursion into the bottoms.

After taking a few photos of the sighting area, we drove the curving backroads until we reached the cemetery. We had been there a few years ago to attend Smokey's graveside service. Smokey was our friend but also a legend unto himself, having first appeared in *The Legend of Boggy Creek* so many years ago. As you know from this book, his life was intimately intertwined with the story of the Fouke Monster both before the movie came out and after, right up until his death in 2016. Jerry and I had met Smokey in the course of our research and had become personal friends. He was a fascinating individual: unique, skilled, and full of tremendous stories.

I pulled my truck into a small church lot across from the cemetery. We were the only ones there, and in fact the only ones in the area. We'd seen no other cars on our drive from the river to the graveyard. We exited the truck and entered the main gate.

We hadn't been to the cemetery since the day of the service, so we didn't know exactly where Smokey's plot was. The cemetery isn't huge, but it is large enough that we had to stroll through quite a few rows of tombstones to find it.

During our search, we came across the graves of several locals who had been prominent in the Fouke legend. Some had appeared in the movie, while others were associated with a sighting or story. It was surreal to see the gravesites of these folks, most of whom we did not have the opportunity to meet in life.

Clouds began to roll in overhead, turning more bruised-gray as they gathered. Within minutes, drops began to fall, gathering like tears on the silent gravestones. If the cemetery seemed isolated and lonely when we arrived in sunlight, it felt even more deserted and lonesome now.

The shower wasn't enough to deter us, however, so we continued our search until we finally located Smokey, who lay resting beneath a respectably sized tombstone with ornate features and an inset photo. Jerry and I stood a moment in silence, both reflecting internally about our times spent with Smokey when he was still with us. It was a bittersweet reflection of good times and exciting stories of the Fouke Monster and his life in the river bottoms.

The rain began to fall harder. We paid our last respects with a few lively quips and verbal goodbyes and began walking back toward the cemetery gate. As we sought a bit of shelter under a row of trees, I noticed a fresh grave. It was that of Mary Beth Searcy. I pointed it out to Jerry and we stopped a moment to pay our respects. Mary Beth had been another prominent figure in the legend, with her story being one of the centerpieces of the old movie. Her passing—which I had already learned of when we were in town—was surely the closing of another chapter in this legendary tale. Mary Beth didn't like to speak of her experience because of years of ridicule, but in the minds of Jerry and I, she was one of the best witnesses. The story of what she saw so many years ago had become famous around the world. She may not have been looking for the limelight, but she had been a key piece in a rich, rural story that has since defined the entire area of Fouke. No matter what she or any of the other witnesses of her era actually saw, it was now part of Arkansas history and thus important to preserve for the generations who have followed the story and for those who will learn of the story in the future.

Jerry and I bid our goodbyes to Mary Beth and exited the cemetery. We got back in the truck and pondered our next move. Had the weather turned on us for the worse? Perhaps not, because within minutes the rain let up and eventually stopped altogether. The sun did not return this time, but the shower had passed. We looked at each other, and without a word, nodded in agreement that we should still head to the woods. If the rain returned, we would deal with it then. I started the truck and set a course toward the upper end of Boggy Creek.

By the time we got to our turnoff, evening was already settling in with a deepening dusk. The bruised clouds still grumbled overhead, helping to usher in a premature twilight. I rolled down my window as we turned off the paved county highway onto the packed dirt of a wildlife management road. The air was slightly cool and filled the cab with the tranquil aroma of trees and fresh rain. A tinge of mystery clung to its moist edges.

I flipped on my brights as the truck tires slowly ground across the dirt and gravel between a canopy of tall trees that covered the entire road. It was like a tunnel where the trees assembled to protect the secrets of the woods beyond. Jerry and I had decided to hike up to a place called Snake Lake, which lies just west of the confluence of Days Creek and Boggy Creek. Though we had hiked and boated most of the territory around it, we'd never actually gone to Snake Lake itself. The subject had come up on our way to Fouke that morning, so it just seemed like the place to go for our night hike. Darkness, threatening rain, thorn-choked bottoms, endless mud, and a place named after potentially venomous reptiles…what could possibly go wrong?

The road near Snake Lake at night
(Photo by Lyle Blackburn)

We came to a turnout where the road dead-ends and rolled to a stop. By now it was almost completely dark, as the last part of the day sank behind the looming trees. Somewhere in the distance we could hear the low snarl of thunder.

Jerry and I changed into our rubber boots and grabbed our flashlights and other essential gear. I snagged my sidearm from the seat and strapped it to my hip. The area was full of feral hogs—though we rarely surprised them—not to mention snakes. For a brief moment we questioned our decision to go ahead with the hike in the uncertain weather, but the rain seemed to be holding off, and it would be awhile before we could make another trip to Fouke. I marked our starting point on my phone's GPS, and we started toward the woods. This would be a piece of cake.

The cake, however, proved to be a thorny recipe. The immediate area around the road was a maze of needled brush interspersed with the rotting remains of huge, fallen trees. Weaving through the deadfall and sharp vines was a challenge. Much of the bottoms here are free of groundcover if you hit the right spot, but in this case we must have entered a cluster that was unusually thick. We forged ahead anyway, weaving a path of least resistance; we must have looked like a couple of drunk hunters stumbling and zigzagging with no purpose.

Finally, after a good distance, we ducked under a huge log that was trapped in suspension and entered an open portion of woods. A soggy carpet of leaves covered the ground before us, but the mass of brambles was gone. I paused to check my GPS. It indicated we had been walking about forty-five degrees off course in our effort to get out of the brush. I recentered our position and pointed in the direction we should have been walking toward Snake Lake.

"It's part of the adventure," I said, jokingly. Jerry agreed as we started across the mushy leaves.

The bottomlands here are some of the most peaceful in the area. The trees are plentiful but spread out enough that it is easy to traverse. As long as you avoid the patches of brambles and areas of standing water, it makes for a pleasant hike. No rocks, no poison ivy, no branches piercing the eyes; just flat, soggy ground and lots of mud.

Jerry and I navigated by the bobbing glow of our headlamps. Occasionally I shined a more powerful flashlight ahead, scanning for dangers and animal eyeshine. With all the moisture from the rain, the beam reflected off the leaves and bog with glints of erratic light. Beyond the range of the flashlight, darkness prevailed. It gathered on all sides like a dark, alien planet.

I held my flashlight still for a moment, focusing on a long stretch of dark water that engulfed the path ahead. We had on tall, waterproof boots, but this appeared too deep and muddy for us to trek straight through. In daylight perhaps we would not have cared. But in the alien darkness, the water looked foreboding, as if it were beckoning us to walk into it.

I used my light to find a higher patch of ground to the left. If we circumnavigated a bit, we should be able to go around the water yet still move in the general direction of Snake Lake. We set out again, slopping through the black mud that lined the edges of the water.

All the while, lightning flashed to the west, illuminating the woods with an eerie backlight. It was followed by grumbles of thunder that were more menacing than loud—like a subwoofer speaker pulsing with deep, animal growls. We just hoped that wasn't a warning of what was to come.

Jerry led with the sloshy sound of his rubber boots freeing themselves from the muck with every step. We swung wide, hit the clear ground, and turned back in the direction of Snake Lake. I checked my GPS to be sure. We had veered off course again due to the detour, but we corrected as we walked further into the hazy darkness of the wooded bayou.

Lightning flashed again, bathing the woods in a quick, bluish light. This time the thunder followed with a louder boom. A storm seemed probable now. We stepped up the pace, hoping we could make it to Snake Lake before the rain. Jerry slogged through a spot of dark water that crept high on his boot. The standing water was often deeper than it looked.

We zigzagged as necessary to avoid more patches of water and stopped after several hundred more yards. I scanned with the flashlight but saw nothing out of the ordinary. It was eerily silent, devoid of the usual frogs, insects, and night birds. For fun, I cupped my hands and belted out my best ape howl. Seconds later, something howled back. Jerry and I looked at each other and waited for it to call out again. When it didn't, I repeated my howl. The thing immediately called back with a short and purposeful whoop. It sounded somewhat like a large bird, but then again not. It could have been some kind of animal. We couldn't really be sure, and it did not respond after further attempts to elicit a response. Such is the nature of the bayou and its slew of unseen denizens.

Light rain began to fall as we slogged through more standing water and jumped a few bug-eaten logs. Lightning flashed and thunder followed in quicker succession, as if a chorus was brewing for a more serious round of storms. I rechecked my GPS to see how close we were to the lake and was puzzled to find that not only had we drifted off course again, but it appeared to be no closer than when we'd left the truck. I chocked it up to the pitfalls of navigating in the dark around a maze of water obstacles, but it was rather odd.

Jerry and I paused as lightning lit up the woods again. In the glow there appeared to be a large, unusually shaped shadow up ahead. I trained my flashlight in its direction, but the beam was not powerful enough to illuminate the spot. The area where the shadow had been was now completely obscured in the rain-soaked darkness. Jerry noticed an odd smell that lingered a few moments in the air. It could have been from an animal or from the Sulphur River; it was impossible to tell.

I looked at Jerry and we both laughed half jokingly and half nervously at the thought that we might not be alone in the storm. It's times like that when all the stories and sighting reports of the Fouke Monster come into perspective. There we were with acres of woods ahead of us, behind us, and all around us; standing in the pitch black except for the weakening battery beams of our head-lamps and a handheld light that could not pierce the full scope of our surroundings. Anything could be hiding out there—watching us. Especially if that something could see better in the dark than we could.

I pulled out my night vision monocular and trained it on the spot ahead where perhaps we saw something. I could only see the residual heat of a few trees. We sloughed off the uneasy feeling that was brewing and continued our trek.

The rain fell harder and more steadily now. The trees shielded us somewhat, but the prolonged exposure to the moisture was be-ginning to soak our clothes. We forged on anyway with an unspo-ken resolve that we needed to make it to Snake Lake, at least for a quick look. We'd come this far already. The outing was starting to feel like a quest for a lost city instead of a hike through Fouke Monster land.

I checked my GPS as we walked, and again it appeared that Snake Lake was no closer, and if anything, further! I recentered our point as the image of the lake spun around as if the GPS was getting confused. I knew it was the result of not being able to travel in a straight line, but still it was strange. On top of that, I imagined us finally arriving only to find a nest of water moccasins slithering about in a black pool. I was beginning to question our sensibility, especially as the rain fell harder.

We scanned the woods again, looking for man-like shadows. We saw nothing, but I suddenly felt as though something *was* out there watching us. I don't get those feelings very often in the woods, but there was something about this situation. Perhaps it was the storm, or perhaps it was that nobody really knew where we had gone. I still had phone signal, but barely. And the GPS had totally lost its mind, spinning our position as if we were orbiting the venomous lake.

Just then, a sudden gust of raindrops swooshed through the trees as the inevitable storm arrived in full force. Jerry and I scrambled to the nearest tree trunk and pressed our backs to it, trying to shield ourselves from the downpour as best we could. It helped, but not much.

"What do you think we should do?" I asked Jerry, not wanting to be the one to give up.

"Whatever you want to do, I'm okay with it," he shouted.

I thought a minute; about the storm soaking my clothes, the sinister snakes waiting for us at the lake, the creature that might be watching us in the woods; and knew the sensible thing was to probably give it up for the night. After a few more moments of heartfelt debate, I shook my head and told Jerry it was time to head back. We would have to conquer Snake Lake under more suitable conditions. The nighttime hike was certainly more adventurous, but there is a time when good sense must prevail.

The rain fell hard and steady as we tried to retrace our steps back to the truck. The GPS kept us on track, but my phone's battery was very low and I had to use it sparingly. In the stormy conditions, it was hard to discern our direction. The boggy bottoms all looked the same, step after muddy step.

After what seemed like an hour of twisting through the mud, water, and brambles, we finally made it back to the wildlife management road, a quarter of a mile from where I'd parked the truck. It wasn't a commendable return journey, but getting out of the thick thorns and increasing mud had become priority.

As we walked the rest of the way down the tree-lined road, Jerry and I began to laugh. We were scratched up, soaked, and covered in mud, but we didn't care. We were in the land of the legend, a place that for both of us provided endless adventure. We had set out on a rather foolhardy mission that night, yet it was all part of the excitement and allure of the Fouke Monster and its famous home. It's an allure that reaches far beyond the two of us. The story has captured the imaginations of hundreds, perhaps thousands, who come to Fouke each year to see its quaint main street, creeks, woods, and scenic bayous. It is a story that captivates all those who watch the original movie again and again and those who learn about the creature for the first time.

The sightings collected in this book are the basis for this captivating Americana tale. They are the lifeblood of a mystery that is as legendary today as it was when the Fouke Monster first made headlines back in 1971. Something is out there, walking the shadowed woods of Fouke. Perhaps it's an undiscovered creature, or perhaps it's something more unexplainable. But whatever it is, it will continue to live on in the details of these truly, extraordinary encounters. Encounters that are often spooky, undeniably mysterious, and forever timeless.

Appendix:
Screen Appearances

The Fouke Monster has been the subject of various feature films, documentaries, and television shows over the years, attesting to the enduring fascination with this case and the potential for dramatizing the incidents. *The Legend of Boggy Creek* is no doubt the centerpiece of the Fouke Monster's on-screen existence, but many other appearances have been launched since then. This section provides a rundown of all the major Boggy Creek-related media.

Feature Films

Return to Boggy Creek (1977)

Return to Boggy Creek was the first of two sequels based on *The Legend of Boggy Creek*. Hoping to capitalize on the success of the original, studio representatives tried numerous times to convince Pierce to direct, but he did not want anything to do with the project. Figuring that the subject matter alone was enough to sell it, the studio decided they would move ahead without Pierce. For the directing task, they enlisted Tom Moore, a relative newcomer who had directed one prior horror movie at the time called *Mark of the Witch*.

Return To Boggy Creek was a departure from the frightening pseudo-documentary style that had worked so well for Pierce. Instead, the producers opted for a more traditional movie approach, incorporating the television star talents of Dawn Wells (*Gilligan's Island*) and Dana Plato (*Different Strokes*). Ultimately the film falls short, coming off more as a heartwarming Disneyesque movie in which the children are the main characters rather than a solid horror film or pseudo documentary.

Boggy Creek II: And the Legend Continues (1985)

By 1984 Pierce had produced eight other films of various kinds, and his interest in the monster subject was not what it was in the early 1970s. He had capitalized on an instance in time at the outset of the Fouke Monster's media heyday, and that was that. As a successful director, he had moved on. But as we are all aware, studio executives are more than willing to sully the name of a classic film in order to milk a few extra bucks out of the franchise. Against his better judgment, Pierce finally relented and agreed to write and direct *Boggy Creek II: And the Legend Continues* (aka *The Barbaric Beast of Boggy Creek Part II*), which was released in 1985.

Pierce ended up regretting his decision to make the film. In a 1997 interview with *Fangoria* magazine, he was quoted as saying, "I really didn't want to do *Boggy Creek II*. I think it's probably my worst picture."

Boggy Creek II was later featured on the award-winning comedy series, *Mystery Science Theater 3000*, which subjected the rather cheesy movie to its wisecracking in episode 1006 of the series.

Boggy Creek: the Legend is True (2011)

Early buzz suggested *Boggy Creek: the Legend is True* was to be a remake of the original *The Legend of Boggy Creek*; however, it is a completely unrelated story set in the fictional town of Boggy Creek, Texas. Even so, the film obviously draws (steals?) influence from Pierce's original with its small-town setting and use of spooky swampscapes—not to mention the ghastly hoard of Southern Sasquatch that pick off the movie's cast one by one. The monsters are certainly reminiscent of the creature from Pierce's film but infinitely more angry and violent, as one would expect in today's horror market. While there are some incredibly memorable scenes, the film regrettably falls short due to a few tiresome elements—including soundtrack, sentimental detours, and extended teenage drama—that continually bog down the potential for solid suspense and horror.

The Legacy of Boggy Creek (2013)

This low-budget, indie movie was originally released under the title *The Skunkape Story*, but it was reedited and released as *The Legacy of Boggy Creek* a few years later. The premise is that it is a direct sequel to Pierce's original film, although it has no sanctioned authority from the estate to do so; in other words, it's a rip-off.

The movie (if we can call it that) begins with a montage of scenes ripped directly from *The Legend of Boggy Creek* to highlight the "attacks" and aggressive behavior of the creature in order to set up the storyline, which starts in 1972. The film even steals the song "Hey Travis Crabtree" and uses it for its beginning credits. Following Pierce's scenes, the movie descends into a dismal affair of low budget, bad acting, and a monster costume that is more suited for a comedy show. Sometimes these low-budget indies can be entertaining for the laugh factor alone, but this one can't even be salvaged in that respect.

Documentaries

The Hunt for Bigfoot (1995)

The Hunt for Bigfoot is a low-budget documentary/movie produced by Jim McCullough Sr. (*Creature From Black Lake*) in association with the late Smokey Crabtree. The movie comments on the Bigfoot phenomenon in general while concentrating on sightings and stories from the Arkansas/Texas area, including several from Fouke. One of the main subjects of the film is Crabtree's controversial "skeleton." Suspected to be the skeletal remains of an actual Fouke Monster, the specimen is examined by two professors of biology and a forensic anthropologist who debate the possibility using various scientific methods.

The *Hunt for Bigfoot* also highlights McCullough's 1976 film, *Creature From Black Lake*, borrowing footage from it to round out the production with what is obviously filler material. The documentary is narrated/hosted by Clu Gulager, a prolific television actor who appeared on hundreds of shows including *Kung Fu*, *Ironside*, and *Knight Rider*, along with a few notable horror movies such as *The Return of The Living Dead*.

The final product, released in 1995, is ultimately a haphazard pseudo documentary that fails to provide much gratification, regarding either the general subject matter or the alleged Fouke Monster skeleton itself. Presumably because of its low-budget production, the documentary never received wide market circulation, making it a rare commodity even for cryptozoology enthusiasts.

FOUKE FACTS: Refer to my *Beast of Boggy Creek* book for the complete story of the "skeleton."

Boggy Creek Monster (2016)

Boggy Creek Monster is a more recent installment in the Boggy Creek legacy. Unlike the films that followed the original, *Boggy Creek Monster* is a thought-provoking documentary that explores the history of the Fouke Monster and the making of *The Legend of Boggy Creek* with haunting scenery shot on location in Fouke, Arkansas.

Produced by Small Town Monsters and based on my own extensive research, the film offers a serious look at the mystery, including never-before-seen interviews with those who were there during the 1970s heyday and those who claim to have encountered the creature in recent years. *Boggy Creek Monster* is directed by Seth Breedlove, a filmmaker from Ohio who has produced a number of high-quality documentaries about similar subjects.

Television

MonsterQuest - "Swamp Stalker" (2009)

The Fouke Monster was the subject of the "Swamp Stalker" episode in Season 3 of this excellent documentary-style television show. The episode features members of the Texas Bigfoot Research Conservancy (now known as the North American Wood Ape Conservancy) as they work to solve the enduring mystery of Sasquatch creatures in the Arkansas-Louisiana-Texas-Oklahoma region. Several eyewitnesses were interviewed in the segment, including Stacy Hudson, who had a spooky encounter along the Sulphur River in October 2000. Jerry Hestand, who wrote the Foreword for this book, can also be seen in the episode.

Lost Tapes - "Southern Sasquatch" (2009)

The Fouke Monster was the basis for the "Southern Sasquatch" episode in Season 2 of this television series. *Lost Tapes* is a "mockumentary" style shows, so while the subject is an actual legend, the events portrayed in the show were fictionalized. The only redeeming aspect is that it features commentary by renowned cryptozoologist Loren Coleman.

Monsters and Mysteries in America - "Fouke Monster" (2013)

The Fouke Monster mystery was examined as part of the "Ozarks" episode in Season 1 of this television series. Even though Fouke is NOT part of the Ozarks—which is a geographic region spanning North Arkansas and Southern Missouri—they grouped it into this area anyway as part of their geographic theme. Aside from the distorted geography, the episode is good. It features the stories of Fouke Monster eyewitnesses, Heather Owen and Doyle Holmes, along with an interview with me.

Finding Bigfoot - "Return to Boggy Creek" (2013)

The Fouke Monster was the focus of the "Return To Boggy Creek" episode that aired in Season 5 of this long-running Animal Planet show. In the episode, the research team visits Fouke, where they learn about the history of *The Legend of Boggy Creek* before heading into the woods to search. The episode features statements from compelling eyewitnesses, such as Doyle Holmes, and local historians, including me. I also accompany the team on their night investigation, which was conducted at the southern end of Mercer Bayou.

Mysteries at the Museum - "Southern Sasquatch" (2014)

Season 6, Episode 7 of this long-running television series featured a "Southern Sasquatch" segment. In the segment, host Don Wildman examines part of a window screen on display at Loren Coleman's International Cryptozoology Museum in Portland, Maine. The screen was donated to the museum by me, and although it came from the Searcy house (as seen in *The Legend of Boggy Creek*), the show implied it was from the Ford house. In keeping with the inaccuracy, some of the facts were incorrect regarding the Ford incidents.

Scene Breakdown: The Legend of Boggy Creek

The following is a breakdown of scenes in Charles B. Pierce's *The Legend of Boggy Creek*, with explanations of the actual reports upon which they were based. The list specifies the *minute:second* where the scene starts in the restored (2019) version of the movie.[iv]

3:12

SCENE: Young boy is running across a field on his way to Fouke to report his mother had seen a "big hairy monster."

Based on an incident that occurred around 1954 in which a mother sent her son on a two-mile run to Fouke to inform the landlord they had seen a large, hairy creature in a field next to their home.

10:16

SCENE: Willie Smith shoots at the monster from his porch.

Based on Mr. Smith's own report in which he claims to have shot at the monster in 1955.

10:44

SCENE: John P. Hixon, owner of the Apache Ranch, describes how he and his son saw the monster running on two legs across their field. The monster appeared to be wounded.

Unknown source. No records of an Apache Ranch can be found.

---

iv *The Legend of Boggy Creek* was restored and remastered in 4K resolution by the George Eastman Museum Film Preservation Service and Pamula Pierce, daughter of director Charles B. Pierce. The restored film was released on Blu-ray and DVD in 2019.

11:10

SCENE: John W. Oates describes how his two prize hogs were killed and dragged into the woods. He suspects the monster.

Based on Mr. Oates's own account in which two of his hogs were killed and subsequently carried off into the woods in 1971. According to Oates, he laid both dead hogs—one weighing eighty pounds and the other seventy pounds—at the edge of his land one evening. The next morning he discovered that both had been picked up and carried off (not dragged). He could still see the imprint of the hogs' hair in the soft dirt of a gopher mound where they had lain. The movie theorized it could have been the work of the monster, but the "monster" was never suspected in real life. Oates lived approximately five miles from Boggy Creek.

14:22

SCENE: Fred Crabtree encounters the monster while hunting in the woods.

Based on Fred's own report in which he claimed to have seen the monster sometime in the 1960s.

15:50

SCENE: James Crabtree encounters the monster near a creek while hunting in the woods.

Based on James's own report in which he claimed to have seen the monster along a creek bank in the 1950s.

17:42

SCENE: Mary Beth Searcy, her sister, and her mother see the creature from their window one night. Their cat is found dead the following morning.

Based on Mary Beth's actual experience in which she looked out the window and saw a large, hairy creature walking on two legs toward their house one evening after dark. The death of the cat, however, was added to the film for dramatic effect.

24:22

SCENE: Teenage deer hunter hears dogs barking and runs out to investigate, taking his shotgun. He encounters the monster, fires twice, and runs for the house, dropping his gun in the process.

Based on a claim made by fourteen-year-old Kenneth Dyas that he had seen the monster in 1965 while deer hunting. Frightened, he shot at the creature and ran for the house. One month prior to Dyas' sighting, fourteen-year-old Lynn Crabtree also had a similar encounter. Lynn fired three times before running. This scene is a blend of the two incidents.

27:04

SCENE: A search party—including men on foot and horseback as well as bloodhounds—sets out to look for the monster.

During the sightings outbreak of the mid-1960s, Smokey Crabtree and others attempted to hunt down the creature. At one point, nearly twenty locals, armed with guns, horses, and tracking dogs, scouted the area but were unable to find it. In 1971, concerned by the new rash of incidents, Miller County Sheriff Leslie Greer organized a new search party to seek out the monster in and around Boggy Creek. Nothing conclusive was ever found.

28:58

SCENE: One member of the search party, a man on horseback, encounters the monster while in the woods alone. Startled, his horse throws him from the saddle.

Based on the report made by Jimmy Cornett, who participated in the hunt. He was riding his horse through the bottoms when some kind of large animal passed nearby, causing his horse to throw him. He could not say whether the animal he saw was a bear, a "gorilla," or something else.

38:38

SCENE: Herb Jones, a man who has lived by himself in the Sulphur River Bottoms for more than twenty years, expresses his disbelief in the monster.

Herb Jones was a real person who lived in a place known as "The Mound" at the southern end of Mercer Bayou. Though there were sightings near his home, Jones never saw the creature himself.

41:50

SCENE: A couple driving along Highway 71 at night see the monster run across the road.

Based on the report made by Mr. and Mrs. D.C. Woods Jr., and Mrs. R.H. Sedgass in May of 1971, in which they saw the monster run across the highway near Boggy Creek.

42:06

SCENE: Monster scares chickens and cows.

Many Fouke area locals suspected the monster was responsible for killing some of their livestock. However, no actual reports of chicken coop raids can be found.

43:22

SCENE: O.H. Kennedy discovers a series of strange, three-toed footprints one morning in Willie Smith's soybean field located near Boggy Creek. Local officials and wildlife experts are called in to investigate.

This incident actually occurred in June of 1971. Mr. Yother Kennedy discovered a series of mysterious footprints in a soybean field, which he leased from Willie Smith. The tracks originated in the woods at one corner of the field and traveled about one hundred and fifty yards before disappearing into the trees on the other side.

47:46

SCENE: Bessie Smith and her children encounter the monster at the edge of their property near the woods.

Based on a sighting reported by Bessie Smith. The exact details of the encounter were not recorded, so it's uncertain how accurately this scene is portrayed. But either way, local sources confirm that Ms. Smith did report a sighting.

50:02

SCENE: Charlie Walraven sees the monster run across the road while driving at night.

Based on a claim made by Charlie Walraven in which he saw a creature run across County Road 9 south of Fouke in about 1967.

51:00

SCENE: Nancy and some friends see the creature from the window of a trailer home.

Based on an incident that occurred in 1971 in which three girls—Chris Rowton, Sherrie Johnson, and Christine Worrell—were alone one night in a trailer home. The trailer was located on County Road 9 near Boggy Creek and Willie Smith's bean field. They heard noises throughout the night as something stalked around on the porch. They never saw anything, but the following day they found "large greasy tracks" left by some unknown animal.

55:20

SCENE: The monster stalks around Howard Walraven's trailer home and is suspected of killing his dog.

Based on a claims and conjecture made by Howard Walraven.

57:00

SCENE: The Ford incidents.

Based on the incidents that occurred in April/May of 1971 at a rental house where the Fords were living at the time on Highway 71. The subsequent newspaper reports by Jim Powell of the *Texarkana Gazette* inspired Charles B. Pierce to make the movie and essentially ignited the Fouke Monster craze of the 1970s.

Sources

Books

Crabtree, J.E. Smokey. *Smokey and the Fouke Monster*. Fouke: Days Creek Production Corporation, 1974.

Crabtree, J.E. Smokey. *Too Close to the Mirror*. Fouke: Days Creek Production Corporation, 2001.

Magazines

Fuller, Curtis. "I See by the Papers." *FATE* March 1972: 24–28.

Jones, Mark and Teresa Ann Smith. "Has Bigfoot Moved to Texas?" *FATE* July 1979: 30–36.

Wooley, John. "The 'Boggy' Man." *Fangoria* #165 Aug. 1997: 13–18.

Movies

The Legend of Boggy Creek. Directed by Charles B. Pierce. DVD/Blu-ray release, Pamula Pierce Productions, LLC, 2018.

Newspapers

Davis, Robert. "Fouke lives with monsters and memories." *Texarkana Gazette* 27 Mar 1988.

Ford, Patricia C. Letter, "The Fords tell 'true' Fouke monster story." *Texarkana Gazette* 22 Sep 1972.

Hutson, Lindel. "Little Rock radio station boosts reward for monster." *Texarkana Gazette* 25 Jun 1971.

Hutson, Lindel. "'Fouke Monster'—What's 'out there' no laughing matter." *Texarkana Gazette* 27 Jun 1971.

Lacy, Bettie. "Monster put Fouke on the map." *Texarkana Gazette* 25 May 1976.

Powell, Jim. "Fouke family terrorized by hairy 'monster.'" *Texarkana Gazette* 3 May 1971.

Powell, Jim. "'Monster' is spotted by Texarkana group." *Texarkana Daily News* 24 May 1971.

Powell, Jim. "'Fouke Monster' seen again." *Texarkana Gazette* 25 May 1971.

Powell, Jim. "'Fouke Monster' legend lives on." *Texarkana Gazette* 23 Jan 1972.

Powell, Jim. "Fouke 'monster' is labeled possible sub-human creature." *Texarkana Gazette* 28 Sep 1972.

Powell, Jim. "Strange footprints spotted again." *Texarkana Gazette* 2 Feb 1974.

Ross, Margaret. "Fouke 'Monster' Had Look-Alikes." *Arkansas Gazette* 27 Jun 1971.

Smith, George. "Fouke put on map." *Texarkana Gazette* 22 Jul 1973.

Staff Writer. "In search of monster." *Texarkana Gazette* May 1971.

Staff Writer. "'Creature' Attacked, Victim Says." *Arkansas Gazette* 4 May 1971.

Staff Writer. "Officers gird for Fouke 'monster hunt.'" *Texarkana Gazette* 7 May 1971.

Staff Writer. "'Monster' sighted; no tracks found." *Texarkana Gazette* 4 Jun 1971.

Staff Writer. "Meandering monster missed once again." *Texarkana Gazette* 6 Jun 1971.

Staff Writer. "Creature's prints found by officers." *Texarkana Gazette* 7 Jun 1971.

Staff Writer. "'Monster' tracks found." *Texarkana Gazette* 15 June 1971.

Staff Writer. "Bounty is offered for 'Fouke Monster.'" *Texarkana Gazette* 23 June 1971.

Staff Writer. "Legendary Monster Becomes Money-Maker." *The Victoria Advocate* 23 Aug 1973.

Staff Writer. "Nonbeliever at Fouke Spots 'Monster' in Cow Pasture." *Arkansas Gazette* 27 Nov. 1973.

Staff Writer. "Texarkana – Wild Beast at Large" *Daily Arkansas Gazette*, 05 Oct 1910.

Thibodeau, Sunni. "The Fouke Monster 30 Years Later." *Texarkana Gazette* 24 June 2001.

West, Bob. "'Monster' hunters facing 'bear facts.'" *Texarkana Gazette* 22 June 1971.

Wicker, Bill. "'Monster' sighting reported." *Texarkana Gazette* 26 Nov. 1973.

Yount, Sheila. "Boggy Creek 'monster' still stalks Fouke folks." *Arkansas Democrat* 22 May 1989.

Webpages

"August 2003 – Track find with photos." *Gulf Coast Bigfoot Research Organization*, www.gcbro.com/ARmiller0007.html

"Bowhunter has early morning encounter while in hunting stand in Sulphur River Wildlife Management Area." *North American Wood Ape Conservancy*, January 26, 2008, http://woodape.org

"Coon hunter and dogs experience close encounter in Sulphur River bottoms between Doddridge and Fouke." *Texas Bigfoot Research Center* (website archive), February 11, 2004, https://web.archive.org/web/20061111140856/http://www.texasbigfoot.com/MillerCoAR1.html

"July 11 1998 – Baby-sitter sees 6 1/2' tall brown swaying animal looking at them." *Gulf Coast Bigfoot Research Organization*, http://gcbro.com/Ark002.htm

"Miller Co. AR sighting report." *Texas Bigfoot Research Center* (website archive), link no longer online.

"November 1984 – Hunter Witnesses the Fouke Monster." *Gulf Coast Bigfoot Research Organization*, www.gcbro.com/ARmiller0009.html

"October 1997 – Man working on car, notices large hair covered creature watching him." *Gulf Coast Bigfoot Research Organization*, http://gcbro.com/Ark001.htm

"Sighting in wheat field near Fouke." *Texas Bigfoot Research Center* (website archive), March 2, 2000, https://web.archive.org/web/20070109105421/http://www.texasbigfoot.com/MillerCoAR.html

"The Return of the Boggy Creek Monster?" *Phantoms and Monsters*, June 10, 2011, www.phantomsandmonsters.com/2011/06/return-of-boggy-creek-monster.html

About the Author

Lyle Blackburn is a native Texan known for his work in writing, music, and film. He is the author of several acclaimed books, including *The Beast of Boggy Creek* and *Sinister Swamps*, whose subject matter reflects his lifelong fascination with cryptid creatures and strange phenomena. Lyle is also the founder of the rock band, Ghoultown, and narrator/co-producer of documentary films including *The Mothman of Point Pleasant* and *Boggy Creek Monster*. Lyle is a frequent guest speaker at cryptozoology and paranormal conferences around the country, and has appeared on numerous television shows such as *Monsters and Mysteries in America*, *Strange Evidence*, and *Finding Bigfoot*.

For more information, visit www.lyleblackburn.com

For the complete, fascinating story of the Fouke Monster and the making of *The Legend of Boggy Creek*, be sure to pick up *The Beast of Boggy Creek*. Available in paperback, hardback, and ebook.

More Books by the Author

The Beast of Boggy Creek:
The True Story of the Fouke Monster

Beyond Boggy Creek:
In Search of the Southern Sasquatch

Lizard Man:
The True Story of the Bishopville Monster

Momo:
The Strange Case of the Missouri Monster

Sinister Swamps:
Monsters and Mysteries from the Mire

Monstro Bizarro:
An Essential Manual of Mysterious Monsters

legend
SCAPE

Made in the USA
Middletown, DE
03 May 2024

53767969R00109